CAPITAL GAINES

CAPITAL GAINES

SMART THINGS I LEARNED DOING STUPID STUFF

CHIP GAINES

W Publishing Group

An Imprint of Thomas Nelson

Published in Nashville, Tennessee, by W Publishing, an imprint of Thomas Nelson.

Thomas Nelson titles may be purchased in bulk for educational, business, fund-raising, or sales promotional use. For information, please e-mail SpecialMarkets@ ThomasNelson.com.

Scripture quotations are taken from the Holy Bible, New International Version®, NIV®. Copyright © 1973, 1978, 1984, 2011 by Biblica, Inc.™ Used by permission of Zondervan. All rights reserved worldwide. www.zondervan.com. The "NIV" and "New International Version" are trademarks registered in the United States Patent and Trademark Office by Biblica, Inc.™

Any Internet addresses, phone numbers, or company or product information printed in this book are offered as a resource and are not intended in any way to be or to imply an endorsement by Thomas Nelson, nor does Thomas Nelson vouch for the existence, content, or services of these sites, phone numbers, companies, or products beyond the life of this book.

Credits:
Page 55 (left photo): John and Maura Stoffer

ISBN 978-0-7852-1633-9 (eBook)

ISBN 978-0-7852-1630-8 (HC)

Library of Congress Cataloging-in-Publication Data
Library of Congress Control Number: 2017950989

Printed in the United States of America
17 18 19 20 21   LSC   10 9 8 7 6 5 4 3 2 1

This book is a love letter . . .

To Jo, of course. You are the best part of me, the
best part of this crazy life we are living.

To Drake, Ella, Duke, and Emmie. You are my greatest
achievement. I look at you four and the whole world feels
cracked open: beautiful and innocent and true.

To my parents and sister and Jo's parents and sisters. We would
not be us apart from you. You have shaped us in so many ways.

To my best friends, each one of you, in every season of my
life. Those days were my training ground for all that was
to come: the good, the bad, and the just plain dumb.

To Magnolia, my favorite team I've ever been on.
There's hope in each of you. The work you do makes me
confident that tomorrow will be even better than today.
And you know what? We're just getting started.

CONTENTS

PART 3: A TIME TO BUILD

FOREWORD BY JOANNA GAINES

As you may have already heard, choosing the cover photo of this book was quite the process. At first, I was like everyone else when I told Chip he needed to pick a "safer" option. I told him no one would get the raw and candid one, and it may be a bit confusing for the actual cover. But the more I heard Chip talk about why he loved this picture so much, the more I started to see his point of view.

For one thing, you can clearly see the wishbone-shaped scar on his forehead. He got that scar after doing something pretty stupid, but the life lesson not only marked him but changed him forever. This experience seems to perfectly embody the subtitle of this book. He also loved the idea that this picture was shot on the farm, on the way to a photoshoot—hat on backward, no makeup, no touch-ups, no fancy camera lights, just a man on his ATV, riding through a pasture.

This reminds me so much of when Chip talks about how life isn't about arriving at the farm; instead it's what happens *on the way* to the farm. For us, the farm is our dream. Most people have an ideal life that they imagine for their future. Something that they work toward and dream of. This is what the farm represents to us.

And yet the point Chip makes is that life didn't start here. We didn't get happier, we didn't become the people we were always meant to be, once we got to the farm. All those things were worked out during the journey that led us there—*that* was the essential part. That was where the endless choices existed, the ones that determined who we were going to be and what kind of story we were going to tell with our lives. You can arrive at your dream a lot of different ways, but you also arrive there as a different version of yourself based on whatever pathway you choose.

I love this book for a lot of reasons, but mostly because it's about what happened *on the way.* Chip is a good man. I could not be more proud to be his wife, antics and all. But he didn't land on the farm and suddenly become the hardworking man of character he is. He, like all of us, was forged in the daily choosing.

This book inspires me once again to live even more intentionally *on the way.* None of us has arrived; we are all just figuring this thing out as we go. But being by Chip's side, I can't help but want to live braver, to dream bigger, and to hold family even closer.

My hope is that when you read this book, you are reminded to not let your mistakes or shortcomings define you. In fact, I hope you see that these are the actual opportunities for you to choose to be the person you always hoped to be.

To enjoying the journey!

—JOANNA

AUTHOR'S NOTE

I've never been one to give luck much credit, but you've got your hands on this book for one reason or another, so let's just assume this has happened for a reason. That said, for this period of time that we're together, I'd like to be your coach and have you on my team! I'll always shoot you straight. To start, your time as a spectator has officially ended —I'm putting you in the race. I want us to work this thing out together. side by side. I'm going to run this leg of the race with you, but get ready because in the end, I'm going to hand you the baton.

Sincerely,

— Chip

ACKNOWLEDGMENTS

Thank you to these creative minds.
Without your help this book would just be a dream.

Jeff Jones | Cover Photo

Billy Jack Brawner III | Art Director

Kelsie Monsen | Cover Art and Graphic Design

Mark Dagostino | Content Direction

Emily Paben, Alissa Neely, and Kaylee Clark |
My Book Club, My Rodeo Clowns

Joanna | For icing my drinks and sharpening my pencils

There is a time for everything,
and a season for every activity under the heavens:

a time to be born and a time to die,
a time to plant and a time to uproot,
a time to kill and a time to heal,
a time to tear down and a time to build,
a time to weep and a time to laugh,
a time to mourn and a time to dance,
a time to scatter stones and a time to gather them,
a time to embrace and a time to refrain from embracing,
a time to search and a time to give up,
a time to keep and a time to throw away,
a time to tear and a time to mend,
a time to be silent and a time to speak,
a time to love and a time to hate,
a time for war and a time for peace.

ECCLESIASTES 3:1–8

PART 1

A TIME TO LEARN

CHAPTER 1

FAILURE TO LAUNCH

I was a normal kid as far as I knew. I didn't feel any different from the kids in my first-grade class. I rode the bus just like everyone else, traded baseball cards during recess, and never let my mom send me to school with a sack lunch on pizza day.

Despite the striking similarities between my classmates and me, one simple fact set us apart: I had yet to learn my ABCs. In case you accidentally glossed over that first paragraph, I was in the *first* grade. I wasn't three or four. I was seven and a half years old. Yet here I was, struggling to read basic sentences.

The first-grade teachers at my elementary school split their classes into four different reading groups. At first, I didn't think anything of it. They were just different teams with cool bird mascots. There were the Eagles, the Falcons, the Blue Jays, and of course the mighty Penguins—the group I was a proud member of. I was the only Penguin in Mrs. Redding's class, although there were definitely a few others scattered throughout the first grade. I'm not sure exactly how she decided who went into which group, but I do know that when it was time to read, the Penguins were ushered out of our individual classrooms and into the gym. And just so you're getting the full picture here: it was a great big gymnasium holding about fifteen kids, some of whom had been diagnosed with actual learning disabilities.

And *me*.

I knew it wasn't "normal" that I couldn't read yet, but it never occurred to me that it was something to be embarrassed about. It's possible that the other kids in my class made fun of me as soon as I skipped off to the gym, but if they did, I never knew it. In fact, the thought of that happening never really crossed my mind. My positive outlook has blinded me to plenty of things over the years. Maybe it also protected me at times from the things that I didn't need to see.

Have you ever heard the phrase *looking at the world through rose-colored glasses*? Well, if there ever were a poster child for this, it would have been me. And even now, I am just fine seeing the world through these lenses. This typically leads me to see the best in people rather than the worst.

I've always had the ability to play things to the positive. Here's how that mind-set played out back in first grade. Kids can be cruel. So looking back, there's a decent chance that at least one of the kids in my class was calling me names while I was off learning to recite my ABCs. But rather than think about these possibilities, I was excited that I was invited to the gym in the first place. Honored even. Look, any chance I got to go to the gymnasium was a win in my book. I loved getting to see the other Penguins. We really only got good time together on Thursday afternoons from one until two forty-five. I'd walk in there and be like, "Whaaat? Where have you guys been? Wait, do you get to hang out in the gym *all* week? How did you score that? Luckies!"

Looking back, I'm not sure if the act of labeling our group as Penguins was random or not, but the symbolism isn't lost on me. All the other bird species in my first-grade reading class could fly—except penguins. Penguins are flightless birds. But that doesn't mean they're "less than." They're actually incredible birds. They do exactly what they're made to do. So while I was happy as a lark to be a Penguin, I sure hope my gym mates never let that label define them. I hope they realized that despite the fact that penguins can't fly, they can do something those other birds can't do.

Penguins can swim.

Some of the greatest success stories of all time come from people who were misunderstood or even miscategorized. Maybe their strengths weren't noticed or valued. Perhaps they got a slow start or went about things in an unusual manner. They somehow didn't fit into the world's narrow definition of what constitutes achievement or success. Here are just a few of them.

FAMOUS FAILURES (PENGUIN EDITION)

- Walt Disney. He was told that he didn't have enough imagination and therefore was fired from his newspaper job at the *Kansas City Star.* Can you believe that? *Walt. Freakin'. Disney.*
- Albert Einstein. The person who allegedly didn't speak until he was four years old and didn't read until he was seven (sound familiar?) basically invented science.
- Oprah Winfrey. She was supposedly fired from her job as a reporter because she couldn't separate her emotions from her work. And wouldn't you know it? That same inability to separate work and emotion was one of the qualities that made us all fall in love with her. That attribute made her stand out among a world of journalists.
- Michael Jordan—the man, the myth, the legend. He was cut from his high school basketball team and still went on to become arguably the greatest basketball player of all time. You know *he* believed he could fly.

I really could share stories like those all day long. They're my favorite kinds of biographies to read and the types of tales I can't help but recount to anyone who will listen. The journey of some underdog slugging and fighting all the way to the top against all odds is infinitely more inspiring to me than the story of a golden child who was born with all the right stuff.

So maybe Mrs. Redding and the other first-grade teachers were on to something. Maybe they intentionally categorized my gym buddies and me as Penguins because they saw something unique in us. Or maybe this is just the way my mind works. I've got a glass-half-full outlook on life. I tend to believe I can truly do or be anything. There are no limits to the things I believe I can accomplish. So yeah, I have a low tolerance for people who tend to disqualify themselves from ever amounting to much before they even try or for people who are constantly their own worst critic.

I realize you didn't sign up for a motivational speaking course, but I'm going to take some liberties here and suggest that if there are external voices telling you that you're nothing special or that you'll never amount to anything, you should probably choose some different people to surround yourself with. And if that unkind voice is your own, I'd like to encourage you to start challenging those thoughts.

You were uniquely created for a purpose. I have no clue what that purpose is for you specifically, but I am perfectly confident that you do, in fact, have one. And you would be wise to stop being your own biggest obstacle. Your purpose is just like mine. It's big, and it's important, and there's no one else anywhere on the planet who can fulfill it.

So quit jacking around and go get after it.

CHAPTER 2

THE BOYS OF SUMMER

I have spent 50 percent of my life throwing a baseball. And not just throwing, but also hitting, taking infield and outfield, and working on the fundamentals of the game. My cleats, my glove, my hat, and that number-16 jersey are the only uniform I've ever known. At one point in my life I genuinely thought sunflower seeds were a major food group.

I didn't care what I wore to class in high school or even college. I could've shown up half-dressed and probably wouldn't have thought twice about it. But the way I cared for every part of that red, white, and blue baseball uniform was a different story—it epitomized my love for the game.

I spent a good chunk of time trying to get my baseball hat to fit just right. To help shape the bill, I would bend it incessantly and wrap multiple rubber bands around it. Then I would run it through the dishwasher a couple of times to make it more pliable. This was a good starting point, but I had to mess with that bill constantly to get it perfect. And that was just the hat.

Before a game, I would spend time scrubbing the grass stains out of my pants to make sure they were bright white. I figured that the cleaner my uniform was going into the game, the more evident my hard work would be afterward. It was like a scorecard to me; the state of my pants by the ninth inning was a direct reflection of how hard I'd played that day. If they were truly filthy, bloody even, I knew I had left everything out there on the field.

And my glove was a whole other story. It was like an extension of myself. Something about it was just magic to me. When I put it on, I felt invincible, like the whole world was at my feet. When I was a kid, my dad had a sporting-goods store, and you can imagine the type of playground it was for sports enthusiasts like Dad and me. I'm telling you, I grew up in that little store. Come spring, my favorite tradition was going to pick out my new glove. I remember trying on every last glove in the shop, and Dad and I would weigh out the pros and cons of each particular one.

Actually landing on which glove to go with was just the beginning, though. The fun part was breaking it in. I'd get home and immediately rub oil into the palm to soften up the leather. I'd start hitting it, fist-to-the-mitt style, trying to get it right. This could go on for hours. The final trick was to roll it up like you would a newspaper, put a ball inside of it, and then tuck it away under the mattress for the night. The antici-pation of waking up the next morning to go try out the new glove for the first time made it almost impossible to sleep. Literally, as soon as the sun even thought about rising, I was out in the front yard breaking in my glove with Dad. We'd toss a ball back and forth, trying to decide how many more nights I'd need to sleep with it under my mattress before it was game ready.

I poured my entire life into that game. Baseball was the center of my universe, this one singular activity around which everything else orbited: school, family, friends, church, weekends, and any amount of free time that I had. Baseball somehow managed to take precedence, and every-thing else fell in line after it. The only reason I even tried in school was so that I could make the grades to play baseball. Education was simply a means to an end.

When baseball was going well, my life was going well. But as soon as one thing went wrong, it seemed as though other areas of my life started to fall apart at the seams. It was a snowball effect, a chain reaction. So I pushed hard to make sure that every aspect of the game was perfect. There was literally no room for error.

My dad and my coach, faithful to the team, as always.

My dad—a consistent, persistent, and faithful coach—was right there with me every step of the way. He taught me that if I would do the hard work and never quit, I would be successful. Dad had played college football, and he was as passionate about *his* sport as I was about mine. He would have loved for me to be more excited about football, but baseball was *my* thing. I chose it, and Dad got on board with me 100 percent. I can't tell you how much I respect him for setting aside his own wishes for mine. His support drove me to work even harder. He encouraged me to hit farther, run faster, and throw harder.

In light of my dad's high expectations, I pushed myself more and more. I woke up earlier and stayed up later. I was dedicated to my dream of playing baseball, and he was my biggest cheerleader. Nothing compared to the satisfaction of making my dad proud. And now, being on the other side of things, I get it. Nothing beats getting to see the smile on any of my kids' faces when one of them gets a hit or steals second.

Baseball was this incredible opportunity, a conduit really, for Dad and me to develop a deep relationship with each other. We spent hours together every single day. The only problem was that we artificially attached ourselves and our relationship to this sport, this one activity. The bond between us was completely built on baseball. It was our cornerstone, the factor on which everything else was based. Love and pride and encouragement were all contingent on how well I played every single game. Literally game by game.

If I was firing on all cylinders, Dad couldn't have been prouder. We'd high-five and recount every play for hours, reminiscing, on cloud nine. But if things didn't go so well, the subsequent hours would look a little different. We'd drive home from the ball field in complete silence. Dad would sometimes storm into the house, slamming the door behind him. And I clearly remember thinking, *My dad doesn't love me because of the way I just played.* I wasn't able to separate my performance from Dad's feelings toward me. Back then, our relationship just hadn't developed beyond the expectation of a perfect performance in the game.

Looking back now, I realize these two things:

1. My dad wanted to be with me. We both loved sports. So if there was a sport to play, he was right there by my side, playing it with me or, at the very least, cheering me on.
2. My father wanted me to be the very best. The very, *very* best. And I love him for that. My dad didn't really have a dad. He was very young when his father chose to leave the family. So every idea my dad had about how to be a father came either from a book or from some other man he looked up to. Without having a direct

example of his own, he just expected of me what he assumed other dads expected from their sons. Or maybe, in his heart, he was just paying me the attention he wished his old man would have paid him, had he chosen to stick around.

I know without a doubt that my dad loved me and was proud of me and did his very best to be a good father. So I'm not complaining. But Dad and I both had a little growing to do, because a relationship centered around just one thing hits drawbacks.

Especially when that one thing goes away.

I've heard that about 6 percent of high school baseball players actually play college ball. And then, of those lucky few, only 8 percent get drafted into the major leagues. I'm no mathematician, but that had to make my chances of playing professional baseball less than half of a percent. But I didn't care. I still lived and breathed that game. To me there was no scenario in which I didn't end up playing college ball and then going pro, no matter what the odds were.

Toward the end of high school, everyone I knew was working hard to build a hefty college application portfolio. They were taking internships, joining academic clubs and debate teams, running for class treasurer (the more easily achieved class officer position), and, on top of all that, going on numerous obligatory college visits.

But not me. I was doing one thing and one thing only: playing baseball. Baseball was my trajectory. It was my plan A, and there was no plan B.

As it turned out, all those hours and days and years of practicing paid off. I actually beat the odds and made it onto a college team. It was surreal to finally be walking into the dream that I had imagined for so long, playing ball for Baylor University in Waco, Texas. But let's not celebrate too soon, because in my sophomore year I was cut, just like that, with no warning whatsoever.

The news hit me like a sucker punch to the gut. And in the following months, I fell into something I can only describe as a deep depression.

The only dream I'd ever had was crushed. The weight of that held me down for the better part of a year.

There are lots of people who don't dream big enough dreams. That has never been my problem. My problem was that my dream was actually too big for me. And when that dream was lost, I was lost too. Dozens of well-meaning friends and family members suggested possible alternatives to help move me beyond my funk. Every single recommendation—all of them—fell flat. I wasn't having any of it.

But hiding away in my dorm room, fooling myself into believing I wasn't made to do anything other than play a game, wasn't going to work forever. Apparently there's a cap to the amount of self-pity time a person gets, because one morning I woke up and realized it was time to snap out of it. The time had come for me to get on with my life.

It wasn't long after that that I remember sitting in a business class and looking out the window at a man riding on a lawn mower. I was mesmerized as I watched the blades of freshly cut grass billow up into the air. Then I thought, *That guy has it all figured out. Why am I sitting in here learning concepts and hypothetical business principles while he is out there grabbing the bull by the horns and actually making it happen?*

It's those seemingly small, fortifying moments in our lives that often end up being the instrumental ones. So as the second hand hit the twelve and signaled the end of class, I closed my spiral notebook, zipped up my backpack, turned my hat around backward, and walked out the door.

I marched right toward that landscaper, confident that he alone held the answers that would save me from my agony and floundering. While I was questioning him a little about his job, I noticed he seemed a bit caught off guard by my interest in his work. I imagined that what he felt in that moment was similar to the way I'd felt in the classroom so many times before. I related to feeling completely unprepared to handle questions fired off by probing professors. After beating around the bush for too long and asking him stupid questions about mowing grass, I was finally able to pry out of him how I'd go about getting a job from the company he worked for.

It wasn't as easy as one might think to get hired by a landscaping company, but I eventually sealed the deal. But let's fast-forward past me mowing a bunch of lawns to the good part.

It was early August when the owner of the landscaping company I'd been working for took me aside to talk. He told me that he thought it would be smart for me to start *my own* landscaping business. Without even meaning to, he drew the same type of confidence out of me that I'd felt when a coach or my dad would call me out and give me advice or encouragement.

That was the very moment when I finally knew what I was going to do for the rest of my life, what I felt truly passionate about—not necessarily lawn care, but dreaming up and starting businesses.

It was the day I knew I was going to be an entrepreneur.

When an uncovered passion sits dormant inside you and then someone calls it out, all of a sudden that's all you can think about. It's like a wildfire being lit by a spark, and the aftermath is all-consuming. I ended up finding a new purpose, a new passion, a new "baseball." Seeing that man ride past my classroom window began my journey toward starting my very first business, the first in a long stream of entrepreneurial ventures.

Getting cut from baseball was something I never saw coming. And looking back, I can see that it could've played out one of several ways.

First possibility: I could have dropped out of college and spent my days lying around the house with my five lazy roommates, eating a sick amount of pizza and getting really good at the video game *RBI Baseball*. My backup plan of moving back in with my parents and having my mom wash my tighty-whities didn't sound so bad either. The passion had been knocked out of me, and there was seemingly nothing good that could fill its place.

Another possibility would've been to suck it up and get a part-time job to occupy my time—just a random job that I didn't care too much about but that paid the bills. Sure, it would have meant giving up on my dreams, but at this point I would've resigned myself to barely getting by.

This option involved zero risk, and there's something really appealing about not rising again after being hurt so profoundly. And although it didn't sound as good as playing Nintendo all day, at least it would get me out of the house.

Another possibility would've been to use every instinct and skill I'd developed over the years, find a new passion, and then go for it. I'd get off of the couch and be okay with hanging up my cleats so that I could pursue something different. And even if this new direction was different from what I'd always dreamed about, I would refuse to quit. Sure, it took me a few months to get my head on straight, but I was resolved to figure this all out. I'm smart enough to know that when you put in the effort and find a new passion and get back on track, good things are bound to happen.

This last scenario is just about the way it turned out. I may have dipped my toes in options one and two, but option three was what all of those years prior had equipped me for. So instead of becoming chronically despondent or detached, I chose a different approach. It took everything inside of me to step up to the plate again, but I did it.

And then I gave it all I had.

Each and every year, as the smell of fresh-cut grass heralds the approach of springtime, baseball season commences, and all is right with the world. The very elements of the game, well known as America's favorite pastime, bring me a certain nostalgia. I am an old soul, and the old-school romanticism of the sport gets me every time. Now, any time I'm in the stands and tear open a bag of sunflower seeds, I can't help but fall in love with the game all over again. But no matter how much I may love the game and the season, I'm always aware that they all must come to an end. In what feels like just a moment, the boys of summer go from being the big men on campus to passing the torch to the boys of fall—and just like that, it's football season.

I have loved baseball as much as anyone, and the lessons it taught me have proved invaluable. But now, in the end, I know it is just a game.

I never, ever thought I would say this, but it's the truth: if I could go back in time and have my life work out differently—not getting cut from the team, actually making it in baseball—I wouldn't do it. I might still fantasize about what that life could have been like, but ultimately I know that God's plan B has been infinitely greater than my plan A ever could have been.

And by the way, my dad was right—every moment of practice was worth it. None of the passion I invested in baseball turned out to be wasted. Moving on to plan B was hard work, to be sure. And I had to relearn what it meant to never quit. But the twenty-one years of my life that I spent pursuing baseball taught me the very things I draw upon in my work today. The discipline I learned on the field helped give me the drive to do whatever it takes to keep building.

Before anything worthwhile can be built, it needs a strong foundation. I believe each life lesson and every opportunity is a building block on which future experiences are built. And that's definitely true of my life in baseball. I'm confident that I wouldn't have been a successful entrepreneur if it weren't for the things I learned in baseball. It was under those bright lights that *grit* and *scrappy* became part of my nature, and fortitude became part of the fiber of my being.

I believed the baseball field was the perfect place to train me as a baseball player, but it turned out to be the perfect training ground for life as an entrepreneur.

That can be true for you too, no matter what your passion is. Every ounce of energy you invest in pursuing your goals will help you grow toward God's plan for you . . . even if you end up somewhere you hadn't counted on.

I can't promise you there won't be any curveballs in your life. But I'm positive that if you do the hard work and never quit—and pick yourself up when things go sideways—good things will be waiting on the other side.

CHAPTER 3

LOST IN TRANSLATION

By the time I was in my mid-twenties, I was knee-deep in three different businesses, and I'd been working with the same group of Mexican guys on all of them. We were a close-knit crew. These were my boys, and something about their culture and work ethic really resonated with me.

It's interesting how when you roll up your sleeves and labor side by side with someone, your stereotypes and assumptions fall away. I found myself preferring to spend time with these guys over my college buddies, and at first, that struck me as strange. Eventually I just owned the fact that the guys I worked with every day were some of my favorite people. Despite their obvious differences, they somehow reminded me of my granddad, J. B.

Granddad lived in a different era, a time when people valued honest hard work. And spending days with these guys was somehow like going back in time and getting to spend even just one more hour with J. B. I had never met a person other than him who could work all day in the blazing hot sun, quite literally from sunup to sundown, and never once complain. But these guys did. And because of that weird connection, I almost grew addicted to spending time with my work buddies.

By "spending time," of course, I mean working. So that's what I did in my twenties. I worked. All the time. With this great crew of Mexican guys I respected deeply.

What did continue to trip me up, though, was how inadequate I was at speaking their language. When we were on job sites together, they did a pretty good job of getting their points across to me. But I was pretty useless at meeting them halfway. I would actually merge English with Spanish and come up with my own unique language—which seemed to confuse everyone even more. Or I would use my hands and face to try to explain to these guys what needed to get done. It was like watching a bad game of charades. Beyond a few basic Spanish terms and a handful of cuss words, I didn't know squat. And for some reason, that really got to me. It seemed that the highest level of respect I could show these men was to learn Spanish so that I could really relate to them and also help them better relate to me.

This lingering desire to learn the language and submerge myself in their culture had long been in the back of my mind. So when I heard about a Spanish immersion program on the coast of Mexico, I was definitely interested. As I looked into the three-month-long program and learned more about it, I felt internally resolved to go for it.

When I shared the idea with my then-girlfriend, Joanna, whom I'd been dating for about six months, I was pleasantly surprised at how positive she was. I actually couldn't believe it. This girl who had played it safe all her life was really supportive of me going to live in a country where I couldn't even ask where my school was. (Looking back, maybe she needed a break or was trying to get rid of me or something.) Her support gave me the nudge I needed to quickly get things in order so I could take off for the summer.

The only problem with getting things in order was that summers were a very important and somewhat complicated season for at least two out of my three businesses.

For instance, in my house-rental business, most of the college kids I rented to went home for summer break, even though they had signed twelve-month leases. This meant that maintenance and day-to-day obligations became a bit simpler in the summer months, but I also had to chase down rent checks more aggressively than I did during the school year when the kids were at least in town.

On top of that, my landscaping business was highly dependent on summer revenue, so there were a lot more moving parts during that time. Any of you who own seasonal businesses can probably relate. We made 65 to 70 percent of our annual revenue during the spring and summer months, and that money was key to our survival in fall and winter.

I decided the only way I could go to Mexico for three months was to leave Jo in charge of my businesses. But that was a lot of pressure. If she screwed up in any way at all, chances were my landscaping business wouldn't make it by the time the third and fourth quarter of the year rolled around. The one relief was that with so many college kids gone, at least my wash-and-fold laundry business would be slow during the summer, so that wouldn't add a lot to Jo's already-full plate.

I called my parents to let them know that I was taking off for three months and would return fluent in Spanish—at least that was the goal. They weren't quite as supportive of this plan as Joanna was.

"Chip, you have multiple businesses," they said. "This isn't college summer vacation anymore, son. Who wouldn't want to go spend a few months on a beach in Mexico? But you have guys who are counting on you to help feed their families now!"

This negativity really threw me for a loop because it was so out of character for my parents. Even though they sometimes wanted me to play it safe, they had also been my biggest cheerleaders and were the ones who had taught me to just go for it in life. For them to question my plans this way, especially now that I was a pretty well-established grown-up, definitely surprised me. But for some reason, the fact that Joanna was on my side really made this thing feel doable. So against my parents' better judgment, but with Jo's support, I signed on with the program. I was headed to Playa del Carmen for just upward of ninety days, and I was going to learn Spanish if it was the very last thing I did.

Joanna was thoughtful enough to throw me a going-away party so that my friends and family could come say good-bye. No fewer than eighty people came to see me off. I thought it was sweet and all, but it also seemed a little strange, given the fact that I was only going to be away for three months. Still, I've never been one to turn down a party. I found myself walking around from person to person, explaining how I couldn't wait to drive down and really learn from the culture. I was really working the crowd, and I gave a pretty touching speech that even made my mom tear up a bit.

Looking back, Jo admits she can't imagine what she was thinking or why she encouraged that kind of behavior. But she did. She even ordered me a cookie cake that said "Adios, Amigo!"

Back then Joanna had a full-time job keeping the books for her dad at his Firestone dealership in Waco. I was always fascinated with how fast she could enter the numbers on the calculator with one hand while flipping through invoices with the other hand. She worked those numbers like a madwoman and wouldn't come up for air until the last invoice was entered. Jo could reconcile that account down to the penny. I had no doubt that when I left for my trip, my businesses were going to be in good hands. I told all of my guys (in very broken Spanish) that if they needed anything pertaining to work, they could find her just up the road at Firestone from eight to five.

Somehow, in all of my excitement about leaving, I didn't really think through the fact that what I was expecting of Jo was going to be very difficult. I knew she had a full-time job, but I severely underestimated the amount of effort it would take for her to keep my businesses afloat for the next three months. But I kept trying to convince myself that I wasn't asking too much of her. All she had to do was . . .

To do's:

Joanna:
- manage three irrigation jobs
- check in on a retaining-wall build
- collect rental checks from 30 students on the
  first of each month
- Deposit those checks
  (also on the first of each month)
- Make sure all subs get paid
- check on the campus laundromat two times per
  week to ensure we aren't short on supplies
- water my plants
- Feed my cows
- Feed my fish

Of course, I also had *allllll* this stuff to do before I left . . .

Chip:
- Pack bag
- Get cash
- Make roadtrip mixtape
- Go to Paradise tan to get my base tan

This may be a good time to fill you in on how I kept up with my finances back then. I was pretty much self-taught in all my operating procedures as a business owner. It should suffice to say that I didn't actually bother to balance a checkbook—not to mention, I never really knew how much money I had in the bank. This was a few years before you could just log in and immediately have your whole financial universe at your fingertips. The way I operated was pretty old-school. I wrote checks when it felt right and didn't write them when it didn't. I kept a wad of cash in my pocket, and I knew things were good if it felt pretty thick. I knew to exercise restraint when it felt a bit slender. These businesses were currently responsible for all the extra *dinero** I was taking with me to make this trip possible.

As if my plan weren't complicated enough, just a few days before I left town I found out that my truck's radiator was overheating. I took it into the repair shop, and they explained that there was a small crack. The radiator would definitely need replacing, but there wasn't money in the budget for a repair like that. So against the advice of the mechanic, I put some radiator sealant in it and prayed the truck would make it to the *playa*.** Just as I was leaving the shop, he reminded me that I'd better take a five-gallon jug of water as backup, just in case. That made sense. I figured that between the sealant and stopping every two hundred miles or so to fill the radiator up with water, I'd (most likely) make it.

So I loaded up the water jug, along with my suitcase and my trusty backpack. Then I grabbed *mi perro****—Shiner, my Chow-mix mutt of a best friend and partner in crime. And off we went, leaky radiator and all.

It was a thirty-six-hour drive to the language school, and Shiner and I had budgeted a full week to get there. We allowed time to make plenty of pit stops along the way and not wear ourselves out with the drive. Every couple hundred miles, I would stop to refill my radiator and top off the five-gallon jug. There always seemed to be a little town at about that point where a lone gas station served my purposes perfectly.

But then something changed. Wouldn't you know it? Twelve hours into the trip, in the middle of the Mexican desert, my truck started to overheat.

I'm not great with cars like Jo's dad, but even I was smart enough to realize something was seriously wrong. The radiator had gone from requiring water every two hundred to three hundred miles to now needing it every thirty miles or so, and I had run out of water. So there I was

---

*   In case you don't know, *dinero* is Spanish for "money."
** Spanish for "beach."
***Spanish for "my dog."

on the side of the road with a steaming car, hood up, in the middle of nowhere. No town. No gas station. There wasn't a soul in sight.

I was feeling great. After all, two things I love most—problem solving and adventure—were both staring me right in the face. Here I was in the middle of nowhere in a foreign country, language-less, with this amazing opportunity to overcome all odds.

I stood on the roof of my truck to get a feel for my situation, and I noticed a small stream that looked to be a ways off. I jumped down, grabbed my lasso,* picked up the empty five-gallon jug, and whistled at Shiner—"C'mon, boy," and we were off.

We walked what seemed to be at least a mile in that hot sun to the stream I'd seen, filled up the jug, and were on our way back to the truck when we happened upon a lone Brahma bull. I've been around lots of cattle in my day, but I can tell you for a fact that there's just something different about a Mexican bull. How we'd managed not to see him on the way to the stream was a moot point. Regardless of how he'd gotten there, he was now between us and the truck—and he was *fired up.*

I must've looked like a straight-up clown, with my mutt, my five-gallon jug of water (which weighed about forty pounds full), and my cheap lasso, running *for my life* from a bull in the middle of God knows where. The more I defended myself against this raging animal, the more precious water I lost. And that dang lasso seemed to be doing more harm than good. The only thing saving me now was Shiner's ferocious defense. By this point the jug had become so light that I could actually use it to strike this beast, which was the equivalent of tickling him with a feather.

We finally made it around him to the other side of that pasture, and in that moment I was honestly just glad to be alive. I quickly poured what was left of the *agua*** into my scalding radiator, and I can still remember the sizzling sound it made. I had drenched the pasture and the bull with

---

* Due to the tight budget, I had been very specific to only spend money on the "essentials," so I had picked this up a few stops back at a five-and-dime.

** "Water."

most of the water my truck needed desperately to make it down the road, and there was no way I was going to cross that bull's path again to go back to that far-off stream.

My vehicle limped along for five miles or so until we happened upon a little gas station. I'm not going to sugarcoat this. Had that station been any further away, both Shiner and I might have died like Pancho and Lefty in the Mexican desert.

Luckily there was an attendant on-site and, due to our inability to communicate, I invited myself to look around the place and rummage through the back of his shop. As I opened drawers, I came across a half-used tube of J-B Weld. If you've never heard of it, it's basically an industrial version of Super Glue. Together the attendant and I took out my radiator, put this magic ointment on the leak, and then reinstalled it. It was clear by the look on the gentleman's face that he wasn't sure whether or not it would work, but it was our best shot.

Considering that the attendant and I weren't sure that the solution we'd come up with was going to work at all, I had to come up with a plan B. So I pulled out my phone card (this was long before cell phones) and used the pay phone at the station to call one of my guys back home. He had told me before I left that if I needed anything at all, he had family in Guanajuato. Now a third of the way into the trip, I knew I had to be getting close to that city in central Mexico.

It wasn't easy with his broken English and my almost nonexistent Spanish, but I managed to explain the situation to him and ask him to alert his family that I would be heading in their direction. It seemed a whole lot less risky to try to make it to Guanajuato than all the way to the beach. I was sure that if I could just get there, I'd be all right.

Somehow I did in fact make it to the front door of my friend's *madre,*[*] hat in hand, just praying that she'd be willing to help. And boy, did she help.

The family didn't know *any* English, and Lord knows I still didn't

---

[*] "Mother."

know much Spanish. Regardless, they received me with open arms—and lots and lots of delicious food. There were fresh corn tortillas, beans like I had never tasted, and chicken they had raised on their small farm. There was also guacamole, homemade pico de gallo, and grilled fresh jalapenos. I realized this meal might very well have represented a week's pay for this beautiful family. We ate and laughed and carried on for hours. What I thought would be a quick pit stop ended up being a three-day stay.

Before I hit the road, I tried to give my buddy's mom a hundred dollars, which at the time would have equated to about a thousand pesos (the equivalent of a month's wages in Mexico). She refused. She grabbed my face with both hands, pulled me in close, and explained adamantly that she didn't want the money. But she did make me promise that as I traveled I would pray for her and her family. And somehow, miracle of miracles, I understood exactly what she was saying.

Something about our time together impressed me in a really meaningful way and gave me exactly what I needed to get on my feet and back on the road. Here I was immersing myself in the Mexican culture and, out of pure necessity, also starting to learn the language.

At the same time, I was now realizing how homesick I had become.

MEANWHILE, BACK IN TEJAS . . .

What I didn't know, of course, was that back in Texas my master plan was starting to unravel. For me, collecting rent checks from less-than-responsible college students had become second nature. But I had not prepared Joanna for the amount of begging and pleading that the process required. Although her talent for bookkeeping was unmatched, I had sorely underprepared her for the events that were about to unfold.

When the rent checks didn't come in, my subcontractors' checks started bouncing. Vendors started calling. And one by one, my subs started tracking Jo down at her dad's tire shop.

It quickly became clear to Joanna why my parents had been a bit opposed to my going to Mexico in the first place. They understood the amount of juggling it took for me to run my businesses, and they knew Joanna wasn't prepared to handle all of these assignments in my absence without months of preparation. On top of that, she was finally coming to understand that the inner workings of my businesses weren't all they were cracked up to be.

I hadn't been fooling her per se. She just never would have guessed that not being able to collect and deposit one month's worth of rent would have caused this much chaos. It had never crossed her mind that I had no backup. No reserve. *Nada.* (That's Spanish for "nothing"!) The money I had taken with me to Mexico was all the money I had in the world.

Not surprisingly, Joanna's father was furious. Back then, while we were dating, I referred to Jo's dad as Mr. Stevens. Though he's Jerry to me now, this story still scares me so much that I'd like to revert to calling him Mr. Stevens for the remainder of the chapter.

For as long as I had known him, Mr. Stevens had been questioning whether I had a legitimate job. And now here were all these people standing in the lobby of his tire shop, demanding the money I owed them. They were making a scene at his place of business, and Joanna was mortified. To say that Mr. Stevens had an impeccable business reputation in town was an understatement, and here I was compromising that.

Thank God this saint of a woman is quick on her feet. She realized exactly what was going on and called my dad in a hurry. Jo actually describes this as the first time she really got to connect with my parents, even though the whole connection was basically the three of them realizing I was delusional.

DE·LU·SION·AL

dəˈlo͞oZH(ə)nəl/

adjective

1. Based on or having faulty judgment; mistaken

"their delusional belief in the project's merits never wavers."[1]

Jo drove to Dallas to have dinner with my mom and dad and to work the whole thing out on my behalf. They were able to access my bank account and temporarily lend me the money to pay my hardworking crew until I got home to collect the missing rent.

I'm really playing it cool here and glossing over some of the emotions, but they were all *mad*. I had deeply disappointed all of the people I most respected: Joanna, my parents, her parents. I'd really screwed this up.

MEANWHILE, BACK IN MEXICO . . .

Things were finally starting to look up. Shiner and I finally made it to Playa del Carmen and were getting acclimated to our new lives at the hostel there. And I found that I actually enjoyed sitting in a classroom and learning this new language, no matter how much work it took. For the first time in my life, being stuck at a desk wasn't downright miserable. It finally clicked with me that maybe the *reason* behind learning this language in the first place far outweighed the pain caused by sitting in a classroom day after day.

I've heard about parents letting their kids take a gap year after high school, and that idea makes a lot of sense to me after my Mexico experience. When you force kids like me to sit in a classroom and "learn," they struggle to get anywhere. But after getting away from school and discovering what they're passionate about, they might actually want to learn. They soak it in. I sometimes wonder why we cram education down kids' throats when the desire to learn comes and goes in life. Forcing it seems like a big waste of time. I say, don't rush it. If it's meant to be, it'll come.

I was about two weeks into class when I aced my first test. I was all excited to find the nearest pay phone and call Jo to tell her about my first A. But when Jo answered the phone, she was already shouting—even before the operator finished informing me that she had accepted this international collect call. (I would like to add that these collect calls were somewhere around twenty dollars a minute, and I was calling her parents' house.) After such an amazing day of learning Spanish on the beach, this was quite the buzzkill.

"Your business is a joke!" she yelled. "All these people are coming to my dad's shop demanding to be paid, and there's no money! Lucky for you, your dad is bailing your sorry butt out. You have *three* days to get back to Texas, or this relationship is over." Her tone made it clear that she was not playin'.

My heart broke. There are hard moments in life when you see yourself for the *tonto** that you are. This all felt so much bigger than a few bounced checks.

Up until that moment, Jo had really respected me and the work that I did. Even if her dad didn't get it, she'd found it admirable and courageous that I was an entrepreneur.

Now, not so much.

Also, I'd spent a good bit of time on the drive to Mexico thinking about when the time might be right to ask Jo's father for her hand in marriage. That dream suddenly felt like it could slip away in a moment. Not to mention, my hope of becoming fluent *en español* was disappearing as quickly as the sun had just melted beneath the horizon of this heavenly place.

The goal that I had set was twofold. Obviously, I wanted to learn the language of my guys, but I also had a feeling that if I could *really* communicate with them, somehow I'd be able to catch a glimpse of the way my granddad thought. And maybe, just maybe, I'd be able to understand him better. So much for both those goals.

Somehow I made it back to Texas in the allotted three days, as promised. By the grace of God, that temporary radiator fix was just enough to get me all the way back home.

I barely remember the drive. I think I probably white-knuckled the steering wheel, sitting straight up in my seat and trying to will myself home even faster than my truck could move. I drove straight to Joanna's

---

* "Fool."

parents' house because I knew she would be there, and I finally pulled into the driveway at nearly midnight. I was deeply dreading what was about to go down, but there was zero chance I could go home and wait 'til morning to face the music.

If you think I look bad on the cover of this book with my ungroomed beard and mullet, you should have seen me then. I looked rough. I hadn't showered in three days. Shiner, ever steadfast, remained right by my side as I walked up to their front door. I carried that stupid lasso with me, hoping my Brahma bull story would serve to lighten the mood.

I quietly tapped on that door, hoping (just a little) that everyone had given up on me and gone to bed. I had begun to second-guess reconciling everything in the middle of the night. Perhaps we should just revisit this whole thing after I'd had some rest and a cold shower.

The pitiful look on my face must have been powerful, because just as Mr. Stevens opened the door, I witnessed his expression melt from anger to grace. I don't know if you've ever read the story in the Bible about the prodigal son,[2] but this homecoming kind of felt like that. There was no party or celebration awaiting me. However, the acceptance and forgiveness I felt from Mr. and Mrs. Stevens and my girlfriend that night was as powerful as it must have felt for the prodigal son upon his return.

MY BASIC SYNOPSIS

THE PRODIGAL SON

This guy leaves home, takes every penny of his
inheritance, and hits the road. He acts like a total punk

---

and then proceeds to quickly blow all of his family's money and becomes destitute. In complete humiliation, he has to go back home and beg his father for forgiveness. When he gets there, he is welcomed back with open arms and a party to celebrate his return.

Simply put, I did not get what I deserved. It was actually amazing in a miraculous kind of way. They could tell by the look of defeat on my face that I was embarrassed. Instead of the school's recommended ninety days, I had only made it a few weeks. So as you can imagine, I was far from fluent, which was the only reason I'd gone to Mexico in the first place. And on top of that, now both my family *and* Joanna's family knew the extreme shortcomings of my businesses. I was operating on very thin margins, and for the first time that became completely evident to everyone. If everything didn't fire on all cylinders, this frail machine I had built would implode almost instantly.

To both my dad and my future father-in-law, paying people on time defined integrity. To them I had just committed a cardinal sin of business—writing checks in hopes that other deposits would come in, robbing Peter to pay Paul, so to speak. They'd also discovered there was no real bookkeeping going on in any of my businesses.

I had a long way to go in regaining their trust and respect, but the grace these men extended to me reframed the very nature of our relationships. It opened the door for the three of us to collaborate on future endeavors. In the coming years they would become my mentors, partners, and investors in various business opportunities.

Before Mexico I sure liked to tell people that I was a businessman and an entrepreneur. But there's a big difference between launching a few businesses and actually building something that's sustainable.

And by that definition, I wasn't operating even one truly successful business.

My intentions in going to Mexico to learn Spanish were sincerely admirable. But to be honest, I was also excited about taking a few months off at the beach. I cared about my businesses and my crew big time, but I was still acting like a kid—and they deserved better than that.

For the first time, while driving that truck home with Shiner by my side, and while feeling the sheer humiliation of being found out, I began to sense the gravity of what it takes to run a business, to glimpse what the life of an entrepreneur actually requires. And it dawned on me that up until then I'd been pretending. An owner of a young business—or in my case *three* businesses—simply *can't* be on a beach two thousand miles away.

It became very clear to me that I had to grow up and become the leader these businesses needed. Or, I thought, maybe it was time for me to cash out and sell them—just count the whole thing as a learning experience.

I'll be honest: cashing out felt like the safest, most logical conclusion. The nice thing about working at some corporation is that you get to go to Mexico as soon as you've saved enough money and accrued enough time off. You don't have to give it a second thought. But when you own a business, all of the responsibility ultimately falls on your shoulders. The buck stops with you, every time.

Perhaps you have to be crazy to choose the life of an entrepreneur, I realized. *But you have to be stupid to choose it without ever counting the cost.*

I look back on that trip as pivotal. I learned some crucial lessons in a short amount of time, and I grew up a lot. After shaking off the doubts, I came back more motivated than ever to dig in and get after it with these businesses of mine. This was the catalyst I needed to create change. If not for that trip, I'm not sure I would have evolved into the businessman I've become.

I also realized I had unintentionally put Jo in a terrible spot. No language acquisition or dream trip was worth that. It became my mission to prove to Jo, my parents, her parents, and myself that I could do this—that I was the real deal, and I wouldn't stop until I made this entrepreneurial dream of mine a reality.

Who could've guessed there was so much to learn from one misguided, bull-fighting, broken-down trip to Mexico?

CHAPTER 4

LEAVE AND CLEAVE

I was twenty-six when Joanna Stevens and I first met. I'd only had a couple of serious relationships by that point. And to be honest, I wasn't really the serious-relationship type, mostly because I was managing three businesses simultaneously and didn't have a ton of extra time. But most of my buddies from various phases of life were already a couple of years into marriage by that point. I think this kind of sped the process along for me, and eventually I started wanting to settle down too. One slight problem, though. I hadn't quite found anyone I wanted to spend the rest of my life with.

The first time I saw Joanna, I knew for sure that I wanted to date her, but I wouldn't say I knew for sure that she was "the one." Several dates in, I still wasn't plotting to buy the ring. And you'd better believe that Jo wasn't exactly planning our wedding either—not after I'd showed up hours late to our first date. But what I did know from day one was that I wanted to spend time with her again. She intrigued me. And I've never stopped feeling that way.

When Jo and I finally got married, we knew we wanted to forge a new path for ourselves. The fact that we ended up with four phenomenal parents, people who love us and support us, is rare. They have sacrificed for us in ways that, looking back, still bring tears to our eyes. We understand how uncommon that is, and we do not take our parents or our upbringings for granted. Since beginning life together, we have wanted to take the best of what each of our parents taught us and the best of our own God-given abilities and weave them together into something that feels just like us.

Jo's parents could have been John and Yoko look-alikes.

I have always found Joanna's parents to be fascinating. They met in Korea back in the 1960s. That's where her mom was born and where her dad was stationed in the Vietnam War. Jo's mom was this firecracker, and honestly she's still that way. She's the kind of woman you love and respect for a lot of reasons. Her bravery and willingness to leave everything she had ever known for the sole purpose of marrying Jo's dad, Jerry, was admirable, to say the least. I can't imagine how scary that must have been, moving to a foreign country and only knowing a handful of words in English.

The two of them were real rebels, genuine hippies—which if you know them today is actually comical. But once they "grew up" and had their three beautiful daughters, they traded in their free spirits for responsibility, order, and safety. And get this: after owning his own Firestone dealership for ten years and then selling it, Jo's dad became a safety manager for Bridgestone/Firestone Corporation. Imagine that. I married the daughter of a *safety manager.*

My parents—the all-American dream.

My mom grew up in a traditional hardworking family, and my father was raised by a single mother. He grew up in borderline poverty, his mom working three jobs just to survive. When my mom and dad got married, they made an unwavering commitment to my sister and me that we would always have a loving, safe place to come home to. They were self-made, middle-class Americans who made a conscious decision to be generous with their time and resources, truly always giving of themselves. This mind-set was really what molded me into the daring, confident person that I am.

They say opposites attract. I don't know what kind of research has been conducted to back up this theory, but if mine and Jo's relationship is any sort of testament, that statement couldn't be any more accurate. During our dating years, it was glaringly obvious how different we were from each other. She's a quiet, detailed, cautiously safe door locker, and I'm a wild, obnoxious, break-every-rule-in-the-book risk taker.

Now, I don't break rules just for the heck of it. I even acknowledge sometimes that they exist for a reason. It's only when the rules are dumb and need breaking to achieve some greater good that I disregard them.

My trip to Mexico really was this make-or-break situation for our relationship. Jo mentioned shortly after that excursion that the time and effort she had invested in my businesses while I was gone was all the convincing she needed to jump in and help out where she knew how. I'm not sure if she just felt sorry for me and my lack of "accounting expertise" or if she was genuinely excited about being a part of the team. Nonetheless, she was in, and I couldn't have been more thrilled.

I felt like I had found my secret weapon. This girl was *sharp*. And good at everything. And she was hot. Jo had spent the past ten years working for her dad, doing his books in the back office of the tire shop. That type of stuff really geeked her out. She loved doing the kinds of things I just couldn't stand to do. So this was the beginning of the very best partnership that I could have ever imagined.

Jo is calculated. She takes into consideration any and all potential collateral damage. I think she must have some big whiteboard in her brain that's operated by little gnomes or something. They're in this war room of sorts, tallying up all the pros and cons, literally playing out every possible scenario to ensure that the best, safest decision is made.

I really do appreciate this trait of hers; I just don't understand it. The caution she exercises in the midst of every last decision has saved us enormous amounts of time, money, and pain over the years, but I just can't bring myself to operate like that.

When it comes to safety and risk, I'm glad that opposites attract. We learned early on in our marriage how to leverage our differences for greater outcomes. I would be out and about purchasing property after property to flip and sell, while Jo was quietly running the numbers, her mind four steps ahead of me. With each potential buy, no matter the risk level or how it could affect our bottom line, Jo always seemed to get behind my half-baked ideas. A few of the times that Jo showed restraint might have cost us something, but mostly her care allowed me to do my thing freely. At the end of the day, we're both stronger for it.

Jo has learned when to raise the little white flag and when to let things play out. And this give-and-take sort of mind-set works for us. She allows me to risk and fly, but when she sees a nosedive in our future, she calls for an emergency landing. And I've learned to trust those little brain gnomes of hers. I know she only calls Mayday when things are looking pretty dicey, so at that point I'd better listen.

Jo and I were easily able to identify our strengths and weaknesses early on. Jo's safe, detail-oriented design eye and my risky, big-picture, get-it-done attitude were the perfect storm of opposites attracting. We are crystal clear on these differences in our strengths, so we know how to run fast in our own lanes and steer clear of each other's. It's really refreshing to feel covered in my weak spots, especially by my wife, of all people, who I trust more than *anyone* else. That is what I would call hitting the jackpot, to say the least.

That's not to say we don't exercise our weaker muscles from time to time. We do. I push Jo toward getting comfortable with big-picture thinking, encouraging her to gain some confidence in her instincts and dreams. And she keeps me focused on small things, because the little details are what keep us on track. But we both walk in authority in the areas of our natural God-given strengths, and that seems to be what makes working together so seamless in our case. As we've learned to harness these opposing characteristics and shore up each other's weaknesses, we've managed to make this working-together thing look pretty easy.

I get that a lot of couples couldn't work together—it's not for everyone. People just figure they'd wring their spouse's neck or something. And if we were to choose to zero in on all of *our* differences, Jo and I could easily drive each other crazy too. But when you recognize what lane you should be operating in and you stay there, the implicated "dangers" of working together start to fall away. It's when you merge lanes and start telling each other what to do that this whole lifestyle we've chosen can start to get complicated.

It's just human nature for couples to turn their insecurities and animosities against each other during life's more challenging seasons. But Jo and I were constantly working on encouraging each other in our harder times because we realized the only way we were going to make it out alive was together.

Both of our parents worked together at various seasons in their lives, and I think that contributes to how natural it feels to us. Jo's mom worked diligently for years to keep costs low at her dad's Firestone dealership. And my mom worked alongside my dad at both their sporting-goods store and flooring company. Having that modeled for us by our parents and seeing how they worked through their differences gave us that much more confidence that this lifestyle could work for us too.

Juggling being co-workers along with being a married couple can feel like walking a tightrope at times. The hardest part for us is turning off the work side of things and focusing on *us*. We have to be really intentional to not talk about business all the time. For example, we have to choose not to discuss project lists, payroll, or an upcoming client on date night. When we get home at the end of the day, the business truly needs to be out of sight and out of mind; our babies and our marriage must be the only things in the world that matter. This has proven to be one of our biggest challenges and is definitely easier said than done. Work-life balance is difficult in general, and we are far from perfect, but we will never stop striving for a healthy relationship in all of its various forms.

We had to get a few good fights under our belt before Jo and I figured out our "big secret" to working together successfully. The key is always giving each other enough slack in the rope to make mistakes. Affording each other a little extra rope has (mostly) equaled smooth sailing for us. So we try to give each other plenty of space. We don't like to corner each other or demand that we talk our problems out right in the heat of the moment.

Giving each other room to stretch and spread our wings also makes our marriage feel spacious. There's room to try things out and change direction. The parameters aren't so tight that we feel suffocated by our relationship, and there's room for both of us to continue to grow and thrive and do our work to the best of our abilities.

The irony here is that while we give each other a lot of emotional and mental space and lots of room relationally to try new things and even to make mistakes, we have much less *physical* space in our relationship than most. Jo and I wake up together. We go to work together, spend all day side by side, and then go to sleep right next to each other. That's a *lot* of togetherness. I wonder if one directly has something to do with the other. Maybe it's when you are always feeling restricted by your spouse, ordered or micromanaged, that the boundary lines of the relationship feel too confining.

It could be because Joanna and I give each other the room to be ourselves, encouraging each other to run and grow beyond our perceived limitations every day, that we love spending nearly every waking moment together. Who wouldn't want to spend all of their time with someone who loves them for who they are and believes the very best about them, who encourages them to fight for their dreams and is the very first one to jump in and fight by their side? And then at the end of that day, they are a safe place to land. (Whoa, writing this out makes me want to spend even more time with Jo.)

I have to admit it took us awhile to figure all this out. When we did our first flip house together, I was doing the painting, sanding the floors, staining wood, and so forth, and Jo was picking out finishes and paint colors and doing the other design things she does. It was her first time to do anything like this and my first time to ever flip a house with a partner. She wanted to micromanage basically every little detail. She questioned why things weren't done yet and gave lots of "tips" on how to do things more efficiently. But I wasn't about to take advice from a first timer on how to do something I'd done for years. We had our first big fight during that job, and I'm pretty sure it took us ten steps backward in our relationship.

After that "little spat," Jo and I realized that we could either pull against each other and create this volatile environment where it would be hard to survive, or we could pull in the same direction. And we've learned that when we pull together, we're a tough team to beat. When Jo and I get into an argument, this tug-of-war concept has often served as a compass of sorts, helping us navigate our way out of our differences. Our "pulling together" mentality helps keep us fighting for the same thing.

Of course, working with a spouse isn't right for everyone. I completely get that. It's a constant fight—fighting for each other, fighting against each other. It seems like it never ends. And on top of that, work can start to become your marriage's centerpiece if you allow it to. But these same principles don't just apply to working together full-time. They apply when you're working together on repainting your house, picking out a new car, or even grocery shopping.

Whether you work together or not, there are going to be opposing forces pushing against you and your marriage. That's a fact. But it's in these sink-or-swim situations that you have the opportunity to be a safe place for your husband or your wife rather than making the struggle even harder. You can fight *for* each other and *with* each other instead of against each other. And when the two of you come face-to-face with resistance, you can pull on the same end of the rope so hard that opposition loses its grip and falls face first into the mud.

Life can be tough, and the world can be cruel and relentless. So far as I can see, the point of marriage is to have a partner, a friend for the long journey ahead. I think by and large people underestimate their spouses. Jo and I have always believed that it is us against the world. It's not that we think everyone is out to get us. But we know that in all the world there is this one singular human who will be on our team every time. Understanding this and protecting it at all costs has become bedrock for our marriage.

It starts with being willing to be seen and known and loved for who you are, as you are. Then you have to be willing to turn around and do the same, loving your spouse in their totality: flaws, blemishes, and quirks included. It's from there that you can begin to forge a trust where creativity and compassion can grow strong. Taking on the world as a unified, fortified duo is not just a romantic notion; it's a powder keg. Together you can set the world on fire.

CHAPTER 5

WRECKED

It's possible you've been admiring the scar on my forehead since the first time you laid eyes on me. It's an awesome scar. I got it right after my first son, Drake, was born.

Jo tends to remember details better than I do, and she claims Drakey was only a few weeks old when it happened. I was thinking he was a little older than that, but I suppose it doesn't matter. What does matter is that the incident that led to the scar was another wake-up call for me.

I'd managed to get myself a brand-new four-wheeler. And let me tell you, for a kid who grew up in Texas, that four-wheeler might as well have been a Ferrari. It was sweet! It was a big investment, too, considering that Jo and I were living in an eight-hundred-square-foot house and had a new baby to feed. But we'd made a little extra cash that month, and I just figured it was time to go out and live the dream, so I bought that four-wheeler without giving it a second thought.

Next thing you know, me and my buddy John took it out and started taking turns, just messing around off-road while our wives hung out and watched. But here's the thing: if Beavis and Butthead and Dumb and Dumber had a baby, John and I would be their love child. (Or maybe it's "love children.") For some reason, we just always pushed each other to do stupid things whenever we were together.

Jo had Drake out there in his little car seat, so maybe I was also showing off a bit for her and my new baby boy.

Anyway, John and I started doing tricks, driving up berms and taking jumps. To be honest, I don't remember exactly what happened next, but at one point I gunned it up an embankment. Maybe I was crazy enough to think I was capable of jumping off the far side and flying through the air like some guy sponsored by Red Bull at the X Games or something. But I think I was just planning to hit the top and spin off to one side, kind of like how a skateboarder might turn at the top of a steep ramp before coming back down.

Only something went wrong.

I gunned it and launched that four-wheeler straight off the other side of the hill—over a sheer cliff that dropped a good twenty feet to the ground. All I remember thinking was, *Good feeling, gone!*

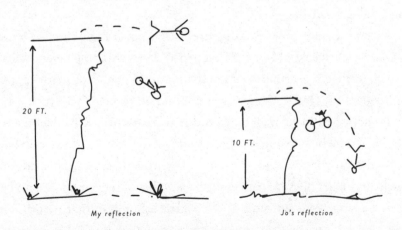

My reflection   Jo's reflection

I tend to embellish, but my honest guess is if I'm six feet tall,
this thing had to be twenty feet. No matter how high that cliff was,
when you land flat on your face, it's a big fall.

Like I said, I don't remember exactly what happened, but the way I remember it is that my body came up off the seat while I held on to the handlebars. The speed forced my feet out behind me, which means I was flying like Superman through the air. I was horizontal to the ground as the four-wheeler slipped out of my hands and shot ahead of me.

I grabbed the back of the seat, just trying to hold on. Now, if I'd managed to pull myself back onto that seat and then land that jump, it would have been legendary! I would have looked like one of those professional motocross drivers, flying through the air on a death-defying leap and then landing with grace while a whole stadium full of people simultaneously chanted,

"CHIP! CHIP! CHIP! CHIP! CHIP!

"CHIP! CHIP! CHIP! CHIP!

"CHIP! CHIP! CHIP!

"CHIP! CHIP!"

Only that's not what happened at all. In a matter of two seconds, the four-wheeler and I went our separate ways. I face-planted into the dirt from nearly twenty feet up. This wasn't like tripping and falling while on the playground. Jo and I both think I must've blacked out in that moment, because I didn't even throw my arms out to protect my face— and I love my face!

It all happened so fast that my reflexes didn't even have a chance to kick in. How the impact didn't break my neck or kill me, I'm still not sure. Heck, maybe I should go ahead and brag about *that*. After all, I'm writing a book, and what better place to talk about how awesome you are than in your own book. You know?

Just seconds after I hit that dirt, I put my fist into the gravel and pushed myself up into a kneeling position. Meanwhile Jo, with the car seat in her arms, and my buddy and his wife came sprinting around the hill to survey the damage. That's when I noticed the blood. In just a matter of seconds, I had managed to create the puddle I was now kneeling in. I pulled my shirt off and pressed it to my forehead.

"#%&$, Chip! We thought you were dead!" John said.

Looking back on all of this, this whole event slightly reminds me of Tuff Hedeman.

MY BASIC SYNOPSIS

RICHARD NEALE "TUFF" HEDEMAN

For those of you who don't follow bull riding, Richard Neale "Tuff" Hedeman is a champion professional bull rider who got slammed in one of the most dramatic accidents in the history of the sport. He was riding in this one rodeo, and an infamous bull named Bodacious kicked so strongly and violently and with such perfect timing that Tuff's face smashed into the hump on that bull's back. The impact broke just about every bone in his face. Then Bodacious kicked Tuff's limp body sky high and sent him slamming down into the dirt like a rag doll. But somehow, as the whole crowd watched in horror, Hedeman got up! With a little help from the rodeo clowns, he walked himself out of the arena—this despite the fact that he would require multiple reconstructive surgeries just to put his face back together. I remember the announcers saying, "What would have killed a normal man didn't even knock Tuff Hedeman out!"

I bet Tuff and I can both attest that when something like that happens, you walk away a changed man.

Okay, back to the scene of the accident. We turned to John's wife, the only medical professional in the group, to see if I needed stitches. I pulled the shirt away from my head, and that woman's knees buckled at the sight of my bloody face. She quickly turned away to hide her gag reflex and croaked out, "Yes, you definitely need stitches."

At the time we had no health insurance. So we called my brother-in-law, David McCall, whose dad was a local doctor and friend in town. It was Sunday, and the clinic was closed, but David's dad said he would meet us there within the next few minutes and help us out. (I probably still owe him some money for fixing my face.)

I'll never forget the sound I heard as Dr. McCall cleaned me up to get ready for stitches.

Tink. Tink. Tink . . .

I strained my eyes to the side trying to see what in the heck was making that noise. I then realized that Dr. McCall was pulling little pieces of gravel out of my face and dropping them into a stainless-steel bowl.

After we left the clinic that day, I remember Jo and I went to get a pair of big sunglasses. I guess I thought if they were obnoxious enough, they'd distract people from the gaping hole in my face. I looked like I'd been run over by a tractor or something.

And *that's* how I wound up with this awesome scar.

My head wound a few weeks after the accident.

Honestly, back in my twenties, the only thing I would have felt after surviving that crash was pride. Sheer, unabashed Texas pride. But I felt something different as I left the hospital that day. After looking into Jo's tear-filled eyes and staring at my beautiful son in his car seat, I felt . . . stupid.

What's wrong with me?

I'd made a habit of pushing the envelope pretty much my whole life. Back in high school, when a group of kids would go climb a bridge to jump into some invariably scary-looking body of water beneath, I'd be the kid who climbed five feet higher than everybody else, just because. I was not about to be outdone.

Risk takers in general are sort of hell-bent on tackling the world and climbing to the top. We don't feel like we're living unless we're walking that edge. There's something about feeling like everything's on the line that makes people like me feel alive. So for most of my life up until that point, I'd felt that if I wasn't redlining it, if I wasn't pushing whatever I was doing to the max, then maybe I'd lost a step or I'd gone soft like everybody else. Or maybe—God forbid—I was just *normal*, a boring, run-of-the-mill kind of guy who'd been reduced to living out an ordinary life. Normal was the complete opposite of what I'd always wanted to be.

But looking at Jo and little Drake after surviving something so dangerous, an entirely new thought flashed through my brain.

I am now carrying precious cargo.

The rush of what used to drive me and make me feel alive was being replaced with the joy I now felt as a husband and father. My wife and my son were a whole lot more important to me than my desire to prove I was man enough to do this or that stupid thing just for fun.

Although I wasn't about to stop thrill seeking altogether, I did realize it was time to grow up. I no longer wanted to purposefully do things that were so outlandish and dangerous they could throw me into life-or-death scenarios. I no longer had the luxury of driving off of a cliff and dying.

What I mean by "luxury" is that, growing up, I imagined I would leave this earth in some dramatic, perhaps mixed-martial-arts sort of way. And I spent a lot of years living off of the rush that recklessness provided. But this big moment made me realize that there's nothing heroic or cool about death by stupidity. And it's a lot harder to take care of a baby and a wife if you wind up in a wheelchair or dead.

These days, I still do stuff that the average person might consider a little risky, but they're not the sort of things where something tragic is likely to happen. The risks I take now are different, more calculated and thought through. But that doesn't mean they aren't plenty exhilarating.

I'm a husband and father now. As such, I'm way more aware of the impact my choices have on other people. I vowed a lot of things to Jo on our wedding day, and I plan to make good on each of those promises.

I'm still a huge advocate for trusting your instincts and taking leaps of faith when it matters. There are plenty of things worth rushing into the unknown for. But don't be dumb. Save your courage for when it counts.

INTERMISSION

*A SHORT STORY ON HOW THIS
BOOK COVER CAME TO BE*

SCARFACE: A MINI-MERCIAL

On top of being an eternal optimist—arguably to a fault—I've always had this sixth sense, or talent or gift or whatever you want to call it. I'm *keenly* aware of my own inner voice. It takes practice to recognize that voice, but once you do, you'll find it to be trustworthy. (Unless, of course, it's always telling you terrible things about yourself, in which case I wouldn't listen to it.)

What do you think about the photo of me on the cover of this book? You like it? I sure hope so. If you don't, that's okay too. But I knew it was "the one" the moment I saw it. I want to take a minute to give you the backstory.

Whenever Jo and I do a photoshoot, it's a big production. A crazy number of people get together and construct these sets or scenes. Hair and makeup people come, and we get fitted for these custom clothes. The lighting equipment required is probably worth as much as my truck.

So on this particular photoshoot, we were in an ATV on the way to the staged area where we would try to get the perfect shot for the book cover, and my buddy Jeff snapped a candid picture of me. This on-the-fly shot, which took zero planning and zero forethought, spoke to me the most out of the hundreds of photos we reviewed at the end of that day. It felt sincere and unexpected and—most important—raw and authentic.

I'm not a huge fan of the circus that is required to make something appear "real." I just like the real kind of real. And I'm probably particularly sensitive about such things these days. So Jeff's photo stood out to me like a ray of light. And the fact that you could see my scar front and center was just the cherry on top.

I am a little obsessed with this scar, you see. It's right smack in the middle of my forehead, and it's just the kind of scar that a guy can be proud of. This was important to me because what I learned when I got this scar really grew me up and changed me forever. It just felt right for this book. In this world of Photoshopped lives and fake news, I just thought that a real photo, snapped in a real pasture by a real person, was in order.

It turned out that *this* photo and two other random options were the final contenders for the book's cover. I posted all three outside my office door and forced everyone who walked by to vote on the one they liked best. And I mean I had everyone vote—people I knew and people I didn't, folks on Instagram, people from out of state, and people from in town too. I had the FedEx guy vote, and I even had a lady vote who had come into the office by mistake, just looking for her dentist.

One option was the photo I had used to announce the launch of this book. It was a funny, fun photo of me jumping through a wall, and it got a great response.

The second was a really handsome picture of me. In my mind I looked just like Ryan Reynolds, only with longer, silkier hair. Even *I* understood the appeal when I first saw it.

Then this third one—what can I say? It was gritty, a tiny bit out of focus, and a little confusing. I was in an all-terrain vehicle wearing a designer suit but with my dirty old hat on. And as far as I was concerned, it was *the one*. But I didn't want to ignore other people's opinions. So I put all three cover options on my door, walked away, and let the chips fall where they may.

Before I knew it, the vote count was 74, 16, and 1. I started doing the math on how many employees were left in the building, and there weren't even enough to make up the difference. So I put together this great sales pitch. And you'd probably assume, since I'm a big, bad business owner, that my employees would concede to my preference without getting smart about it. Especially since it's *my* book.

But if you assumed that, you'd be wrong. The vast majority of them preferred the first two photos.

IIII IIII IIII IIII
IIII IIII IIII IIII IIII
IIII IIII IIII IIII
IIII IIII

IIII IIII IIII I

I

Brock Murphy,
my personal assistant,
I mean the director of PR

Someone mentioned that I looked
like I was sitting on the toilet so I
threw this option out altogether.

I listened. I really did. And then—*bam!* I yanked the Magnolia Home by Joanna Gaines™ rug right out from underneath their feet and chose the third option. They never saw it coming. If they know one thing about me by now, it's that I won't go against my gut, especially for the cover of my juicy tell-all.

I wish you would've seen those people's faces when I carried in the cover options and announced the winner. This coup d'état* ended up being a great lesson for my team in going with your gut. Yes, somehow I see myself as the freedom fighter in this scenario.

It's very important to take other people's opinions into consideration. It's crucial, even. You can't operate in a vacuum. But in the end, it's your life. It's your work. The conclusions you come to ultimately reflect you, and it's critical that it reflects *you* honestly.

So here's the point: learn to hear your inner voice, and then trust it. Get a sense of when it's offering suggestions and when it's stating a mandate. And when it states a mandate, listen to what it's telling you to do. Then act fast and don't waste time second-guessing yourself.

Confidence in your intuition takes practice. You need to exercise it. Experiment with it. Try to visualize what you want to happen, because if you can't at least imagine it first, you can forget actually making it happen. Then, once you can "see" it, it's time to act.

The only difference between a painter and an aspiring painter is that willingness to put those inner urges into action. So get to it! Just get started and believe you *can*, then go from there. Eventually you'll find that hearing and following your inner voice becomes second nature.

Today I'd ask you, what voice are you going to listen to? Everyone has opinions, and that's good. It's what makes the world go around. But sometimes all the opinions can keep us from doing what only we can do.

In the end, only I could have known how this book cover was supposed to feel. I needed every opinion I got, if only to confirm what my inner voice was saying all along. But once I listened to what others had to say, the final decision had to be mine.

If I ever become really famous, I hope that kids dress up as me for Halloween, just like they do with Harry Potter. But instead of the lightning-bolt scar, they'll need a big wishbone-shaped scar in the middle of their foreheads. That would be pretty cool!

---

* *Coup d'état*, also called a *coup*, is "the sudden, violent overthrow of an existing government by a small group"—or in this case, an individual. (Encyclopedia Britannica Online, s. v. "coup d'état," accessed July 23, 2017, https://www.britannica.com/topic/coup-detat.)

THE END

*NOW BACK TO OUR REGULARLY
SCHEDULED PROGRAMMING*

PART 2

A TIME TO GROW

==

CHAPTER 6

FEAR-LESS

Life has never been particularly scary to me. Between Jo and me, we've learned a lot of lessons the hard way. Riding out the turbulence, even living through a few nosedives, has allowed us to see that fear isn't part of how we're willing to live our lives. We've experienced some of what people deem as the "worst possible scenarios" together, and we've come out on the other side. For as long as we've been married, Jo and I have made a habit of just trying things out and hoping for the best. Because we're not afraid to fail, fear has lost its power over us.

This is a really important point to understand: when you aren't trying to avoid failure, fear loses its foothold. The courage to take a chance is half the battle. The other half? Viewing failure as a teacher and not an enemy.

But not all fear is about failure. What if someone hurts us or takes advantage of us or steals from us? That's always a possibility, but we can't let fear be the deciding factor that holds us back.

I have a long history of believing the best about people. I never fear a stranger without good, verifiable evidence, and usually not even after that. If faith in others bites me in the butt, so be it—and Lord knows, it has a few times. I'll give you a couple of examples.

In college my roommate, Riley, and I used to leave our front door unlocked all the time. We didn't live in a great area of town, but it just wasn't our style to give it that much thought. I guess we believed we had more important things to worry ourselves with.

We left for Thanksgiving break, and I think each of us thought the other had locked up. We came back from that week out of town to find our apartment wiped clean. Everything was gone—down to the Fruity Pebbles cereal in the pantry. We probably would've been a lot more upset about it had we lost anything of sentimental value. But honestly, it was just a bunch of junk college kids seemed to acquire. We got some insurance money, and we bought all this cool stuff we wanted—a big TV, a tower full of CDs, a great surround-sound system. Our place became a twenty-year-old's paradise.

Then we left for Christmas break. My roommate thought I locked the door; I thought he did. And—you guessed it—they cleaned us out again. All of that new stuff, less than a month old, was gone.

It's kind of laughable now. You'd think we would have learned our lesson. But apparently not, because some years after that my truck was stolen out of our driveway because I left the keys in the ignition. Maybe that sounds like a one-time thing, but that's not exactly accurate. It's just something I've always done—not necessarily on purpose, but I guess you could classify it as a bad habit of mine. I will admit that I haven't really tried to change it, because I've always kind of assumed the odds were slim that someone would steal my car, but the odds were pretty good that one of my buddies would need to borrow it.

Joke's on me. Turned out my buddies never needed to borrow my vehicle, but somebody did want to steal it.

And here's another one that hurts a little more. Back when Jo had her original Magnolia Market, which we nicknamed the Little Shop on Bosque, I hired a couple of neighborhood kids who couldn't have been older than fifteen. The area where the retail store was located wasn't exactly the best part of town, so when they came by asking to help, there was no way I was saying no. I was actually proud that they wanted to earn money, so I immediately put them to work. They primarily unpacked boxes, helped clean and pick up around the property, and did a few other odd jobs. This went on for weeks.

One day after closing I went out back to mow the lawn, which ended up taking a good bit of time. I left the boys inside the shop with a punch list of closing duties like sweeping the floors and cleaning the bathroom. When I came back in to tell them they could call it a day, I was surprised to see they were already gone. Initially, I just kind of thought, *Wow, good work, boys—way to get after it.* It took me a while to realize that something was off, but I didn't fully understand what had happened until Jo came back the next morning and discovered the cash drawer was completely empty. After that night, we never saw those boys again.

Now, here's where believing the best about people comes in. I can judge myself for my unwillingness to lock things up, but who am I to judge the people who actually stole from me? I'm going to leave that part to be worked out between them and their Maker. I like to believe that the truck thieves had somewhere they *really* needed to be and my apartment robber(s) were *really hard up* for a CD collection and some fresh undies.

What still gets me, though, is the kids from the Little Shop on Bosque. Those boys worked so hard all that time, and then out of the blue they made this one bad decision. That leads me to think they had an urgent need for that money. I would have gladly given it to them if only they'd had the courage to ask for it.

The point is, rather than changing how I operate, I choose to think better of people than they might even think of themselves. Even if I got all up in arms about these things, who am I to jump to conclusions? I don't know their story, so I'm not going to make snap judgments about them.

All that to say, I will probably continue doing these same things that I have always done. Some might say I'm irresponsible, being a poor steward of my things, or tempting fate. The reality is, it's just what I've always done. And I refuse to let my life be driven by fear of what others might do or what might happen to me.

Now, I'm not recommending that you do as I do. I actually married a door-locking, alarm-setting, large-dog-purchasing woman, and these days I feel like I live in Fort Knox. But in my heart nothing has changed. I want to keep my family safe, and I want to use my resources wisely, but fear is not part of the equation, not even a little bit.

The people I love are the only things I hold precious. And my fretting over our safety or future or even our health won't add a day to our lives—but it might well diminish the days that we've got.

I'm going to get on a bit of a soapbox now, and I hope you'll bear with me. If I ever run for public office one day, there's a good chance my stump speech will be about making it illegal to live in fear. The reason I'm so passionate about this topic is that fear will literally ruin every single facet of your life; it cripples everything. You know how hurt people hurt people? Well, scared people scare people. And thus, the cycle of fear continues on.

Coming at you in 2020.

Fact: life isn't safe. You could do A, B, and C all perfectly right, and then *bam!* All of a sudden D will show up, and D wasn't even on the guest list.

A lot of people spend their days walking in fear of failure, pain, or even death. But things like disease or war still find their way past triple-locked doors. No alarm system can keep these things away. And I just don't see the point in putting energy into doing what isn't possible in the first place.

So like I said, life isn't scary to me. I don't sit around and allow the what-ifs and the worst-case scenarios to control me. There are so many things that can knock us down, so why waste one minute worrying about what we can't control? I intentionally choose to think about things differently.

I realized a long time ago that if you open the door to fear, even just a little, then it all comes flooding in. President Franklin D. Roosevelt famously said, "The only thing we have to fear is fear itself," and on that, he and I can wholeheartedly agree.

My point is this: For the rest of your days, you can live in fear of what *could* happen. You can walk instead of run, drive instead of fly, or leave the big city and move out to the suburbs. But you simply cannot protect yourself from the things beyond your control.

I don't want to make this too depressing or anything, but right now, at this very minute . . .

- There are nuclear weapons being tested[1] and chemical weapons being further developed,[2] while a quarter of humanity lives without electricity.[3]
- There are more than a hundred different varieties of cancer, with many different causes, but no dependable cure.[4] And that's just cancer. An estimated sixty-eight thousand different human diseases are classified by the World Health Organization.[5]
- There are more than one hundred fifty million orphans in the world,[6] and nearly eight million children die of preventable diseases every year (diarrhea, pneumonia, malaria) because they are too poor to afford treatment.[7] To say that even more explicitly, twenty-nine thousand kids under five years old die because of poverty *every day.*[8]

- If the conspiracy theorists have gotten any of this right, the air we breathe[9] and the water we drink[10] are slowly poisoning us each day thanks to some epic, global assault against the human race.

You see where I'm going? If we let every potential threat out there dictate how we feel, there's a decent chance we'll all curl up into the fetal position and never leave the house. Sometimes too much information is immobilizing.

I vote that instead of fretting about the problems in this world, we all become part of the solutions. This happens through our willingness to make small, brave decisions. No one is born a hero. It takes a lifetime of courageous choices to get there. So quit dodging hard things. When you make the choice to duck left to avoid something scary, you could miss a beautiful opportunity on the right.

To this day, I'm still surprised and so proud that Jo had the *huevos rancheros* to up and move to New York City during college. She went there to pursue her dream of broadcast journalism. That didn't pan out. But she left New York with the beginnings of an even bigger dream.

Jo was a bit homesick in New York, but she felt a sense of peace when she would wander through the little home-decor boutiques she found throughout the city. Those cozy shops inspired her so much that she began to imagine a way to create something like them for herself. And when we got married, this was one of the first things I encouraged her to do.

And Jo went for it! It didn't matter that we had no money or that the timing wasn't just right or that she had no idea what she was doing. That shop of her dreams was going to be a reality—and all because of that beautiful risk she'd taken in going to New York.

Of course we don't always know whether the decisions we make are going to be life altering or not. But I'd argue that *every* choice we make, big or small, points us down a particular life path. It's like those "Choose Your Own Adventure" books that all the kids read when I was growing up. One choice leads to another, and the results can be amazing. But if we spend our time focusing on what *might* go wrong or how we *could* fail, then we're likely to talk ourselves out of doing anything altogether—without even stopping to consider what the cost of saying no might be. Swaddling ourselves up in our security blankets completely restricts our ability to take courageously bold steps.

I have this short friend, Becker. He's six years old and wise beyond his height. Last night, at an impromptu gathering of friends, he requested that the attendees sit as he explained the rules for the evening. "At a dance party, even if you are just a little bit embarrassed, you still have to dance." If this small fry isn't a modern-day prophet, I'm not sure who is.

If you don't ask out the girl (or guy), you risk ending up alone, too scared to pursue a relationship. If the thought of traveling to a foreign country terrifies you and you bow to that, you miss out on experiencing the big, exciting world that's out there just waiting on you to discover it. Say you never apply for (or accept) a job that feels beyond your capabilities, but instead choose to stay in an easy, safe position that never requires you to grow, change, or build something that matters. That's not just sad for you; it's sad for the rest of us, because *we need what you have to give.*

The other thing about the presence of fear in the process of decision making is that it can severely cloud your judgment. Fear dressed up as wisdom provides poor counsel. It lures you into thinking that if you will just trust it, it will afford you some level of control.

But guess what? You're not in control. So I'm calling bull on that illusion. It's time for a wake-up call. Maybe a little cold water in the face couldn't hurt.

Life isn't safe, remember.

But life can be wonderful if you choose adventure rather than fear.

I get where these fearful tendencies are coming from, I really do. Humanity has, by and large, come to the conclusion that the world is getting worse and worse every day and that people are ultimately bad. No wonder everyone's scared to death.

Life feels altogether different when your perception shifts, though. It's amazing how gorgeous the landscape of life looks when we choose to

believe that all people have good in them and every situation has potential for a positive outcome. It may be buried or dormant, but I truly
believe it's there—most likely waiting for someone to look for it, to help
unearth it, to expect it, maybe even to *demand* it.

We're all bumbling through life just trying to figure things out. Is
any of us perfect? Not a chance. Are some of us up to no good? For sure.
Do we get taken advantage of? Of course—probably me more than most.
But I don't want to ever stop believing in people or taking chances on
life just because I'm afraid things might not pan out the way I'd hoped.

I'm convinced that seeing the bad in the world and in people isn't
difficult or wise or insightful—it's lazy. Finding the good in every scenario typically takes a lot more work. But the rewards of peace and joy
and hope are so worth the effort.

It's possible that the perspective shift I'm describing may be more
difficult for you than for me. Maybe you have one of those certified pho-
bias. Let's see, there's amychophobia, the fear of being scratched (I get
that). Then there's phagophobia, the fear of swallowing (not sure what
the day-to-day looks like for you people), and hypnophobia, the fear of
sleep (can't relate to that one), to name a few.

Or maybe you have involuntary fear stemming from pain or a trauma
in your past. You never know when some experience will trigger the
flight-or-fight response in you and leave you shaken.

If you are an extreme case like this, there's no need to cold-turkey
it. Maybe baby steps are what's in order. You might even need to seek
help from a counselor or physician. But whoever you are, whatever your
situation, I believe you can still make the choice to move farther away
from fear.

How about we *all* start with choosing a little more courage today
than we had yesterday?

There's a scene in this movie that I watched with the kids, *We Bought
a Zoo*, where the dad gives his son an amazing piece of advice. This is the
direct quote. I know because I made Ella get up and pause the movie so
I could write it down. Then I played it back a second time: "Sometimes

all you need is 20 seconds of insane courage. Just, literally 20 seconds of just embarrassing bravery. And I promise you, something great will come of it."[11]

That's it. That's the stuff. Each time you muster up what it takes and go for it, the next go-round becomes that much easier. Real and important changes begin with small, courageous acts.

It's never too late in your story to take a step away from fear. And the good news is that both optimism and courage are contagious. No hand washing necessary. Simply catch and spread.

CHAPTER 7

BABY STEPS

I remember it like it was yesterday. Sometime near midnight Jo grabbed my arm and whispered, "I need to tell you something." Back in those days, that sentence was typically followed by, "I'm pregnant," two simple words that normally had the power to thrill me. But because Jo was *already* pregnant with number two, I knew this couldn't be the case. Ella, our second child, would be born in a few months, and we were still getting used to the idea of what life would be like with *two* babies. I flipped the bedside lamp on and sat up so Joanna could tell me what was going on.

"I think it's time to close down the shop," she said, her voice matter-of-fact. I looked over at her in complete disbelief, expecting tears. But she didn't look sad, and there was no disappointment that I could read on her face. Still, I knew how hard this must have been for her to actually say out loud.

Now, to give you some context, the original Magnolia store we had opened back in 2003 was just starting to hum along. Jo was in her element, and she had developed a unique style that attracted many locals. She had built up a solid customer base and had finally found a rhythm that was so fun to watch and support.

My first instinct was to pat her on the knee and tell her to get some rest, that we'd talk about it in the morning. I honestly thought she'd just had a long day and wasn't thinking clearly. Back then she spent most of her waking hours at the Little Shop with Drake, then a toddler, at her feet. Drake was still waking in the night and she wasn't getting much sleep. I knew she was completely exhausted, and I didn't want her to make a big decision like that while she was running on empty.

But Joanna didn't want to wait until morning. So my next instinct was to give her advice. I've always been the type of person who swoops in to save the day, so I felt it was my responsibility to throw out a couple of suggestions to keep this dream of hers going. Not that Jo ever needed my saving, but I just couldn't help myself. I mentioned finding a couple of part-time employees, one to help out during the morning shift and one for the afternoons so Jo could spend more time at home during the day.

She looked at me with those determined eyes of hers and shook her head. "No, Chip. It's time. I feel it in my gut."

This shop wasn't a hobby for Jo. It was her life. Joanna's work ethic is a blend of her father's drive and her mother's persistence. That combination made my wife a workhorse who was just plain fun to watch. She was so passionate about every little detail. As soon as the shop closed at five, Jo would take up the hunt for something new and unique to add to her inventory. She would run into antique stores and thrift shops ten minutes before they closed and grab broken-down pieces of furniture that she'd bring home and pour her heart into restoring once Drake was in bed. My wife was a one-woman retail machine, and nothing could stop her.

Until now.

Until this.

Joanna is an all-or-nothing kind of woman. This characteristic made it hard for her to balance home and work and feel like she was doing either one with excellence. Just doing the bare minimum at the store wasn't going to solve the problem. To be able to give the babies her full attention, she knew she'd have to give up the shop.

By this point, I was wide awake, and I knew Jo wasn't just going to let this one go. At that time, the shop provided at least half of our household income, a necessary supplement to my work flipping and building houses, so the idea of shutting it down sounded not only risky but, to some extent, downright foolish. But she was clearly serious, so we got out of bed, moved the conversation to the kitchen, and quickly started game planning for our future.

It's not typical for Jo to come to me with a potentially life-altering decision already made. She's more likely to start a conversation so we can hammer out the possibilities together. But when she intuitively "hears" something and senses it's from God, there's no changing her mind or talking her out of it. I wouldn't dare try. Even back then, when we'd only been married three years, I understood that when Jo heard God in a way that seemed weightier than usual, her discernment of His voice was usually right on.

Jo and I *both* have strong instincts and enjoy the process of due diligence, but if we specifically feel like God has initiated something, we do not hesitate.

Sitting there at the kitchen table, pen and paper in hand, Jo and I spent the night and well into the wee hours of the morning strategizing how to announce the shop's closing and sell through the inventory. We also brainstormed ways to make up for the income loss we were guaranteed to experience. Jo threw out the idea of reviving something she had done a couple of times before—hosting one-day sales in our home. Jo would stock up on unique furniture pieces and home decor items and literally set up shop in every room of our house. These home sales had been so successful that every last piece typically disappeared by noon. Jo suggested doing four of these a year, and that really started to seem like a workable option.

We eventually headed to bed a couple of hours before Drake got up, feeling nervous and expectant for this new season we were about to enter into. I wanted to be just as supportive of Jo closing the shop as I had been of her opening it back in 2003. And I really was genuinely happy for her. Joanna's dream had been to build Magnolia Market into something she was proud of, and she had exceeded those expectations. Now, three years later, she had a new dream, one she cared about so passionately that she was willing to let go of her beloved retail store. She yearned to be home with those babies.

Sometimes the quiet decisions—the ones reached at two in the morning at the kitchen table—are the ones you look back on with the most fondness. That momentous night with Jojo set off a chain reaction of events that quite literally led us to where we are today. And it all happened because Jo said yes to that feeling in her gut, that quiet voice telling her it was time for a new dream. I had never been more proud of her. She and I both knew she was taking a God-sized risk, but she wasn't afraid.

Within two months Joanna had sold all of her inventory, settled the books, and let her vendors know she was closing up shop. The two days that stand out the most to Jo from the Little Shop were the first day she opened (she was a nervous wreck) and the day she closed the doors for the last time. No matter how difficult it was to walk away that afternoon, Joanna knew it was the right thing for us. She took a deep breath, turned the key, and walked away from that little shop on the corner, filled with nothing but peace about her decision to say good-bye.

Throughout the following year, I could tell Jo loved being at home, focusing on our children. It seemed like a weight had been lifted off of her shoulders. It was a great year, an amazing year, and I think Jo must have subconsciously willed Pinterest into existence that year with the sheer force of her creativity. This was the time when she really learned to cook, clean, garden, scrapbook, craft, and do all the inventive stuff she now loves. I knew the kids loved having her home around the clock, but sometimes I considered using my body as a human shield to protect those young lives from their mom's endless creativity and energy and her capacity to do a million small projects all at once.

To give you an idea of what I mean, today Joanna Stevens Gaines is the cohost of a top national reality television show, on which she personally designs up to eighteen custom homes a season. In her off time, she manages every last detail of a retail and design empire while lovingly feeding and clothing and caring for four children under twelve—and keeping up with me. And this is the same woman who focused all of that creative talent and energy into staying home with our two small children. No wonder she got a bit restless!

Both Joanna and I agree that there's not a more noble calling than staying home with your kids. But this woman had far too much energy for this to be our long-term plan. Our poor children. She plumb wore those young'uns out! By year two, Joanna was jumping in on my building projects just to keep from bedazzling the kids.

Then, just like that, Joanna was pregnant again with our third baby—our second boy, Duke. I specifically remember during that pregnancy how much she missed having her own true creative outlet. She started asking me to bring home more and more construction plans, and she would sit at the dining room table during the kids' nap time and work on the design, the layout, and the functionality of these spaces. She had a real gift for imagining herself in these people's homes (not in a creepy way). She would pretend it was her own bathroom, kitchen, or living room, and that made her see and notice things I never would've considered.

She would come up with these quirky ideas that at the time I honestly thought sounded pretty dumb. *What do you mean we're going tear off the drywall and leave these old planks exposed? Ship–what? And you think painting this old mantel and then fastening it to the wall will make it feel like a fireplace? That's not going to feel cozy; it's going to look bad, and then we'll be left with huge holes in that wall. And you want to install an antique door to a pantry? The homeowners are going to hate that!*

But they didn't. In fact, they *loved* it. Because Jo had spent the last few years as the owner of a home-decor shop, and because she'd spent countless hours studying her customers' spaces at their request, she had become an expert at finding unique ways to fill homes with meaning instead of just stuff. She actually knew what she was doing, and people were eating it up. Joanna put herself in the middle of the process and made herself an invaluable member of the construction team—a much-needed addition to our crew of clueless men who had zero background and little sense about all that interior-design stuff.

And so Joanna Gaines, Designer, was born, but not in some fancy design school or as the underpaid intern of some high-priced interior decorator. She'd been born with the eye for it. She'd worked at it and practiced and fine-tuned her natural ability. And eventually she became this unstoppable, incredibly gifted, and highly skilled design mogul.

As we started preparing for baby Duke's arrival in 2008, we also began feeling the effect of the national housing crisis. The homes we had bought to flip were now sitting on the market months longer than expected. When they didn't sell, we were forced to rent them out or even owner finance—anything to cover the banknote. I realized that if we didn't reinvent ourselves, we weren't going to make it. And for me the latter wasn't an option.

I realized quickly that we needed to diversify. So we jumped into residential and commercial remodeling. Before, we'd built a reputation on flip homes, investment properties, and a handful of new builds, but this was a different world. In the risky financial climate, people were choosing to take whatever money they would have put as a down payment for a new house and spend it on their existing homes. For the time being, people were sticking with what they had and improving their current living situations. That meant updating kitchens and baths, taking down walls to create larger rooms—all kinds of projects to make what people already owned work better for them.

The remodeling business wasn't exactly the answer to our prayers from a financial standpoint. Things were still tight. But Jo trusted me, and she knew that no matter what, we were going to figure it out. I've always been wily, and I love a good challenge, so I wasn't wasting much time standing around and shaking in my boots. I was all about forward motion.

Joanna's thirtieth birthday was coming up, and I'd told her in the past that since she had done such a good job surprising me for *my* thirtieth, I would find a way to beat her with an even bigger surprise. The only problem at this point was that we didn't have much expendable income at the time. That was not going to stop me, of course, but it was definitely a hurdle. So one Saturday afternoon I picked up the phone and started calling around town to see if anyone had ideas.

My first call was to the owners of our local magazine, *The Wacoan*. I wanted to know how much it would cost to take out a "Happy Birthday" ad in their next month's issue. The answer was $695. Even with just about no extra cash floating around, that price seemed like a bargain to pull off surprising Jo. It was the ultimate way to wish Jo a happy birthday in style. But while I had them on the phone, it hit me that every month *The Wacoan* published a "Who's Who" column, which was pretty much just an "events of that month" recap. So, being quick on my feet, I promptly invited the magazine to cover Jo's big thirtieth birthday bash.

"Wait," they asked, "*who* is this again?" But I skipped right over that question and redirected them onto something that was sure to make them bite. I let them know that there was going to be a full-on red carpet with all kinds of prominent Wacoans in attendance. They bought it.

The only problem was . . . I didn't know any prominent Wacoans. But that little detail didn't faze me. Now that I had the magazine on board, my plan had grown from a "Happy Thirtieth Birthday, Jo!" ad in the magazine to a full-fledged surprise party.

I was still going to do the ad, but I now intended to use it as a bartering chip with all of the vendors I was going to have help me put this thing together. My impromptu plan was to use the ad to give a big shout-out to everyone who donated their services for the event. I convinced these vendors that the publicity would be way more valuable to them than their typical fee would be. The exposure they'd get at such a noteworthy event would be well worth their bartering cost.

Jo tracked down the actual ad. Here it is.

With this logic I managed to secure a location and hire a photographer, a live band, a full coffee bar, a caterer, a florist, and—oh, wait, did I mention I somehow got the mayor there too? I called her office a week before the event and explained to her assistant that this was going to be the party of the year. I also mentioned that all of the "who's who" of Waco were going to be there. I knew, of course, that my "who's who" list probably looked a little different from hers. But it wasn't as if anybody was asking for the guest list, so I just kept my cards close to my chest on that one.

On the evening of the surprise party, Jo thought she was going to a small garden party with close friends. I was happy to let her think that. I hadn't managed to actually surprise her with anything since our engagement, so I was due.

Then the limo driver arrived, and Jo's surprise started to unfold.

When we reached the venue, you would have thought we were the most notable couple in Waco, Texas. The red carpet rolled out, and photographers snapped pictures. It was the closest thing this town had ever seen to paparazzi. Inside there were twinkling lights everywhere, and the band was playing Frank Sinatra. There were gorgeous floral arrangements on every table and silver trays full of fancy food at every turn.

Somehow I was able to pull off the surprise of a lifetime on that $695 budget, and I swear it was a nicer party than our wedding reception. Being all but broke wasn't going to stop me from making Jo feel like the most important woman in the world that night.

Even to this day, we look back at pictures and can't believe that I pulled off that kind of party. It very well could have been the last of our money, and I wouldn't have cared a bit. She was worth it. In those days, broke or not, we somehow always seemed to find a way to celebrate the milestones.

The two of us at the big surprise party. (Joanna thought she was going to a quaint garden party with a small handful of friends.)

After the first few kids, I started to feel as though all I had to do was look at Jo and she'd get pregnant. When she conceived Emmie, our very last baby, I'm pretty sure I just winked in her general direction. Baby number four was born in 2010, and that little girl brought us more joy and fullness than we ever could have anticipated. It seemed that our adventurous and brave Emmie Kay was the final puzzle piece to complete our family of six.

During this time in our lives, with four kids under six, Joanna and I kept doing mostly commercial and residential renovations, with a side of flip and rent houses. It was a trying and exhausting season, but one that strengthened our patience and our prayers and taught us how to dream even bigger. And finally, after much hard work, things started to turn around. In fact, it was during that time that the TV show was born. We filmed the *Fixer Upper* pilot in 2013 and the first episode aired in early 2014.

Right about that time, Jo and I took a break and went to Arizona for a couple of days. I dropped her off at a little nursery adjacent to a park so she could look around, get inspired, and maybe take a load off while I ran a few errands. When I came to pick her up an hour or so later, Jo was already waiting out in the gravel parking lot for me.

If I know anything about Joanna Gaines, it's that something's not quite right if she's able to leave a plant store with not one single piece of greenery. So I swung the door of my truck open, confused by the lack of shrubbery in her hands, and pretty much instantly recognized an all-too-familiar look on Jo's face.

"Chip, I've got something to tell you," she said.

Baby number five?

Nope.

"I think it's time to reopen the shop."

In the single hour that I'd left her there in the nursery, she'd heard that familiar voice quietly urging her again. As we sat in the car and Jo sketched out an action plan for reopening, I remembered back to that night when she'd told me it was time to close the shop. Now here she was, more excited than ever, and 100 percent sure that this had been God's plan since the very beginning.

About three months later, Magnolia Market reopened in that very same building it had originally called home. How's that for full circle?

I've spent a lot of my time thinking about life and thinking about business, and I've noticed that in both, sometimes it feels like you have to take steps backward in order to make large leaps forward. That was certainly true in the season that started with Joanna's decision to close her shop. We made the choice to love each other through one of the most challenging moments in our relationship and our work. While I tackled the business side of things, Joanna singlehandedly ran our household from a place of love and patience and a willingness to go above and beyond for our family. She added an element to our construction team that gave Magnolia Homes an edge over every other construction company in town. We weathered an economic downturn by changing our business focus from flipping houses to personalized home renovations, and we persevered until it started working. Our family grew from two to four kiddos. We closed and then reopened Magnolia Market. We both turned thirty, and we did it in style. And oh, yes—we got ready to go on TV!

There isn't a business plan out there that can predict all of life's uncertainties or the ups and downs of unknown economies. But what we learned in this eight-year "in-between" season was how to trust our gut(s) and when to go with our instincts. We recognized fear, adversity, challenge, hesitation, loss, and chaos as the hurdles that they are. These things were tough, but they weren't impossible. We cleared some of them with ease, and with others we fell hard on our faces but kept on going.

Nobody remembers if you cross the finish line bruised and bloody. They just remember that you stayed the course. Don't get hung up on how ugly the race may have looked. In the end, all that matters is that you finish.

CHAPTER 8

GROWING PAINS

I can't say for sure what Magnolia looks like from the perspective of someone on the outside, because it's my life's work. I am inundated with it day in and day out. But this multifaceted business was our first baby. In the early years it needed to be cared for, protected, and nurtured. It really did require every ounce of energy from us.

I realize that not everyone who reads this book owns a business, but I'm sure many of you have either had or been around small children. You understand the amount of attention they need, especially early on. Honestly, starting a business is not that much different. Magnolia has grown from a tiny start-up, the smallest of small businesses, to a mid-sized small business. Someday I believe it will be great, with far-reaching effects and influence. But for now it's more like a young ballplayer with tons and tons of potential but a long way to go to be considered one of the best.

When several hundred employees depend on your company to succeed in order to put food on their tables, that's something that bears a whole lot of weight; it's an extreme amount of pressure. But to Jo and me it's also an honor and a privilege. We love it and the people who work with us, and we consider it our responsibility to pour every last drop of our heart and soul into this business.

But maybe I should back up here . . .

In 2014, after Jo made the decision to reopen Magnolia Market, she really didn't know if it would sink or soar. Those are the details we spent hours worrying about. But her motivation for opening her shop in the first place wasn't to make it succeed. We realized early on that every minute spent worrying about that was a minute wasted. This was her hard-earned moment to do the thing that she had been passionate about since her homesick days in New York, and I wanted to help her any way I could. But it took a bit of juggling to get everything in place.

As I've said, we made the decision to reopen the Market in that same building on Bosque Boulevard, which we still owned. We had tried to sell it, but all the deals fell through, so we had used it as an office for Magnolia Homes. Our design people and project managers were still working there in 2014, but we had to make room for Jo to do her thing in the front space of the building. So we moved the designers and managers into the offices in the back half of that building.

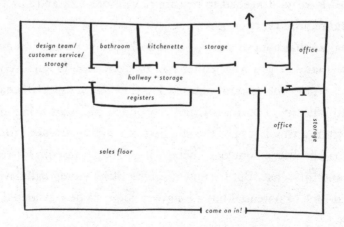

A sketch of the Little Shop on Bosque, our first Magnolia Market.
It didn't take long for us to be bursting at the seams.

Now, by "back half" I am talking about a few hundred square feet. This space was more of an oversized closet or storage room than an office. It had no windows and therefore no natural light. But these early employees, these precious souls, didn't bat an eye. They didn't complain once. One of the real reasons we are here today, one of the reasons we made it through so many tough times, is because those early team members were all-in.

I'm getting ahead of myself again here, but it's worth pointing out that these employees really did create the mold for future hires. They gave us a template, a profile to ensure that all our employees would have this same attitude. They exemplified courage, selflessness, determination, and a sincere passion for this young business. They didn't care about the glory or the spotlight or even seeing the light of day. They cared about getting things done for the greater good and being trustworthy stewards of this business that we'd all poured so much blood, sweat, and tears into.

The days, weeks, and months that followed the reopening of Magnolia Market were a whirlwind. We were simultaneously filming season one of *Fixer Upper*, and without the help of this team that surrounded us, we wouldn't have survived even two weeks.

Then, pretty soon after the shop reopened, we launched our online store. I guess we've always been workaholics to some extent, because we just couldn't leave well enough alone. It was a major high point to see those first seeds we'd sown with this little shop finally come to fruition. With every online order that came in, Joanna became more and more excited and emboldened to make this thing work. She was so energized by this part of the business that our team took notice and started helping out as much as they could, wherever they could, even if it meant staying late to help pack and ship boxes. These nights would turn into all-night pizza parties. Our folks would even invite their roommates and their friends because there was so much energy and excitement that even outsiders wanted to be a part of this.

These were such good times, and all of those involved remember this season with such fond memories. Everyone was learning how to service the online customers. We were using shoeboxes, vendor boxes—whatever we could find—to pack our products in, and we padded each package with crumpled newspaper.

I think we have known for a long time that there is something unusual about our business. Not a week goes by that we haven't seen some sort of bona fide miracle take place somewhere at Magnolia. In fact, so many remarkable things happen all the time that it has simply become a part of our culture, our DNA. We expect God to show up, and He does—over and over again.

In those days, our shipping headquarters was basically a big metal barn in the backyard of the Little Shop, and our "warehouse" was a slew of white carnival-looking tents set up around the perimeter of the barn to (inadequately) protect our product from the elements.

There was one night back in 2014 that a tornado watch fell over our county. Jo and I were out of town for the weekend, so our employees banded together and called an emergency "all hands on deck" meeting to save the product under the tents from getting completely ruined. Every last one of them showed up at the Little Shop in the middle of the night, ready to help. Having no other choice, they stuffed everything they could first into the barn and then into all available floor space inside the store. When they ran out of room there, they started stuffing items into their cars, just doing their best to keep the inventory from getting damaged.

That night it stormed like nothing you've ever seen, and Jo and I heard the news where we were staying. Unable to leave, we just prayed we'd come back the next day to find our shop still standing. First thing the next morning, we beat a path home and showed up to survey the damage. Only two thousand dollars' worth of inventory had been ruined.

We weren't happy about that loss, of course, but we knew it could easily have been ten times that. Our hearts were overwhelmed to realize our employees had come to our shop in the middle of the night, in the pouring rain, just to protect our little business.

Shortly after that, we got ourselves an oversized shed to store our backstock product (product kept on hand in the back-of-house that is set aside to replenish what we sell through on the sales floor). We named it Big Blue—and we soon outgrew it. Then we got another, smaller shed and a few storage pods to make room for more lamps and candles and other stuff Jo sold in the store. We outgrew them. Soon we were back to setting up white carnival tents, and this time they covered the entire backyard. It looked like some sort of traveling-camp-revival setup. And you guessed it, we outgrew every single one of those too.

Things were moving at such a breakneck speed that we didn't even have time to read *How to Build a Retail Empire for Dummies* (if such a book existed). We were just doing well enough to realize that we needed boxes. *And* packing peanuts. *And* people to put those peanuts in the boxes. *And* customer service reps to answer complaints about the peanuts.

Emmie trying to ship Ella to Virginia.

So many products were being shipped out of the backyard of that little shop that FedEx had to back up an eighteen-wheeler to our make-shift warehouse every day just to handle the onslaught of orders that the online store was producing. The long and short of it was that we were finally making real money. And I've never met an entrepreneur who wouldn't agree that making money feels good—especially coming out of the kind of drought we'd been in.

By this point, obviously our Magnolia Homes design team had moved to a rented office space, because there was no place for any productive work inside that madhouse. And our three customer service reps moved into that same oversized closet that the design people had occupied. Our store manager and purchasing agent were working out of the only two "real" offices in the place, which probably totaled thirty to thirty-five square feet together. There wasn't even space for a door to swing open and shut, so they hung curtains instead.

Looking back and recounting all of this is actually hilarious. I really don't know how we even got from one end of the hallway to the other without tripping over one another or the quick-to-grab restock product that lined the walls.

Did I mention that the whole place had only one bathroom? I'm pretty certain that every single unfavorable Yelp review we ever had in those early years was due to the fact that we had to reserve the bathroom for our employees (with the exception of kids and emergencies). Even with that restriction, a line would form down the tiny back hallway leading to the john. That's because at that point, maybe four or five months into this gig, in addition to the customer service reps, purchasing agent, store manager, shop workers, and Jo, at any given moment we also had ten to twelve people in the backyard packing boxes. That's more than twenty people who all loved coffee and shared a single bathroom. Exciting times indeed.

In January 2015 it became clear that shipping out of the Little Shop simply wasn't sustainable anymore. The brick and mortar store needed the product storage space for restocking, and we had maxed out our available space for new packers to work. So we started looking for a real warehouse.

The one we chose was near downtown, about ten minutes away from the shop. The minute Jo walked in, she knew it was the one because of its old, familiar, distinct smell. Turns out this vacant warehouse had been previously occupied by a tire wholesaler. Jo vaguely remembered picking up inventory there for her dad back in her Firestone days. This building reminded her of those nostalgic times spent at her daddy's tire shop, which made it feel like it was meant to be. So just like that, we bought it.

The empty warehouse before we moved in.

It felt surreal to own an entire warehouse. It felt like we were growing up.

The day we moved in, it snowed in Waco, Texas—which happens about once every three years if we're lucky. The snow seemed like some sort of sign, like the weather was celebrating this new season with us.

Rented box trucks drove back and forth that day, moving product from the Little Shop to the warehouse until every last bit of our online store's inventory was transferred over. I remember walking around the new warehouse and realizing that even with what felt like a ton of pallets of inventory, they still only took up a fraction of the available space. Maybe we'd overdone it with this new building. It seemed massive. How would we ever fill it?

But wouldn't you know it—the online store started going bananas. It turned out that the "oversized" warehouse was in fact a godsend. We did all we could just to keep up. We now had a staff of six customer service reps who worked full-time. We had at least ten people picking orders and twenty more packing them.

The very first Shipapalooza at the warehouse.

On more than one occasion we had to host a "Shipapalooza," in which every single Magnolia employee worked in the warehouse packing boxes morning, noon, and night just to keep up with the online orders. They were rewarded with overtime pay and all the barbecue they could eat, but I honestly believe these people would've done it for free. It seemed that each and every last one of our employees was just as excited as we were for this sudden boom in business. It felt like those late-night pizza parties in the backyard of the Little Shop. Something about the rush of it all never got old. And having so many people in our corner was the best part. We were reminded at every turn that we couldn't do this alone.

It wasn't just the online business that was growing. The Little Shop on Bosque continued to do well, too, and for the first time in our lives, we were drowning in something other than debt. This time, it was customers. People from all over the country were stopping into Magnolia Market to stock up on candles and oversized clocks, cake stands, and Magnolia wreaths. We had four or five full-time people manning the registers and restocking the floor. And on weekends we had interns and even friends of ours show up to help. On Saturdays we zoned someone to stand at the front door and control how many people could come in. *Space was tight.* Eventually it got so crazy that we set up a large white tent out in the front parking lot to display product.

THE LITTLE SHOP ON BOSQUE

TRAFFIC JAM

By the way, the Little Shop had a parking lot big enough for eight or nine cars max. And on a busy day, we could have thirty or forty customer cars needing a place to park at one time—not to mention the employees' vehicles. Behind the Little Shop was a residential neighborhood without much street parking, and Bosque Boulevard is a busy four-lane road, so there just wasn't a safe place to get in and out of a car. But we were fortunate enough to be located right next to a church that allowed our customers to use their lot Monday through Saturday. We had decided early on to be closed on Sundays, no matter what, so this worked out perfectly for everyone. I don't know if Magnolia Market would have survived without that gracious church. That fact alone is enough to be enormously thankful for the generosity of others.

Despite the obvious growing pains, we were keeping our heads above water. Operations at the warehouse were coming together, and we'd hired a few extra people to run the Little Shop as well. We were all chugging along when our store manager, Alissa, who had been with us from the beginning, asked, "Don't you think it's time to create a marketing department?" And then she offered to run it.

What would we do with a marketing department?

That seemed like a complete luxury to me. We still had real fires to put out and real problems to solve. I was nervous that if I lost this key employee to some "feel good" role like marketing, I might miss out on the practical, crucial, day-to-day tasks she'd been responsible for. But despite my reservation, I told her to go for it.

So Alissa carved out a little corner of the warehouse for her new team. She pulled a girl from customer service who'd been spending part of her time posting on social media, and she pulled one of the assistant managers at the store who'd had some experience doing marketing for a minor-league baseball team. And voila—our marketing team was born.

Alissa is still with us today. It's amazing to see how some of these original hires have grown to become valuable members of our executive team.

Prior to this we didn't really have official departments established, other than maybe customer service, the crew that ran the Little Shop team, and the warehouse folks. It was really more like a group of people who were all working together to accomplish the same goal. Back then, one person might be doing four or five different assignments at one time. When needs would present themselves, a group of us would peel off to make sure they were taken care of.

Once Alissa set up her marketing team, however, it didn't take long for people across the company to start forming actual departments. Groups of different employees clicked together to form our purchasing, operations, accounting, merchandising, visuals, photography, e-commerce, and human resource departments.

Over the next few months, even with the boom in business, money was always tight. We were trying to bankroll the new warehouse and all of the new products we were buying to keep up with demand. So although it seemed like we were rocking and rolling—and we were!—there was very little margin for error.

Every single employee had multiple responsibilities. We even hung a "chore chart" in the break room. Each employee took their turn vacuuming, wiping down windows, mopping, cleaning bathrooms, and taking the trash out to the dumpster. There's just something about picking up trash and taking it to the dumpster. To me it's always seemed like the most basic, most humble task in any operation. I always knew that if I ever got too important to pick up trash, my priorities had gotten out of whack. What I loved about this crew of ours was that as they buzzed around doing important work that mattered, they were also aware of the little things like picking up trash.

Not one person complained. No one ever thought certain jobs were beneath their pay grade. Our people just stepped right up to the plate and did whatever was needed. It wasn't unusual for a member of the customer service team, on the phone with a customer who was waiting for their order, to go out into the warehouse to dig through boxes and stacks of product, then pick and pack that order personally.

I also remember a time when someone called customer service and offered to give me a pig. I didn't really know what to do other than accept the offer. So we sent three people from the Magnolia team out to get the pig and bring it back to our farm we had bought just outside of town.

Whatever it took.

Texas heat can be brutal, and the warehouse wasn't air-conditioned. During the summer of 2015 we decided to stop shipping candles temporarily because they were quite literally melting in the boxes before we could get them shipped. Somebody lost their office for a few weeks so that the candles could be stored inside the air-conditioned space and we could continue to fulfill orders.

Another highlight of those exciting warehouse days was an all-out mouse infestation. They chewed their way into boxes of small wreaths, had babies, and built little mouse apartments out of every last one of them.

And then there was the photography "studio." When our photography team needed Web site product photos, they would set up operation in the entryway of that warehouse. We had built a shiplap wall there, and they snapped pictures right there in front of it, using anyone passing by to help. Some poor person would be walking by on an important mission, only to be recruited to help hold up product so we could get the perfect shot. But perfect proved to be a moving target. We usually had to take multiple shots because you could invariably see someone's face, legs, or arms in the picture.

Thanks, Jonathan, Alissa, and Rachel!

And back to those freakin' packing peanuts. We found out through our customers how bad Styrofoam peanuts were for the environment, so we invested in this amazing machine that converted used boxes into packing materials. What we didn't consider was how much shipping would cost to ship with all of that heavy cardboard packing material. We were always weighing options in those days. Cost versus quality. Time versus savings. Energy versus efficiency. It was a constant battle.

The point I'm making here is that as we grew the challenges grew with us. But we turned just about every situation into a learning opportunity. We even brought in a warehouse operations consultant to help us shed new light on issues we couldn't seem to get right. The only problem was even the experts couldn't find a business just like Magnolia Market to model ourselves after, and so we really were navigating unchartered waters.

By the end of 2015, our brand-new warehouse was busting at the seams, just like our Little Shop on Bosque. The same building that had felt so big to us just one year before now seemed entirely too small. And it was crystal clear to us that this newfound nationwide buzz around Magnolia Market wasn't slowing down.

By then we'd signed on for a few more seasons of the show, and we knew it had given us a national platform that was only going to get bigger. People were taking notice, which made Waco a destination for the first time in as long as anyone could remember. We were seeing the beginning of a renaissance in our city, and we knew it was time for the Little Shop to find a bigger place to call home.

CHAPTER 9

THE LONG GAME

We finally had our heads above water.

We were busy shooting the second season of our show and had just settled our family into the farmhouse—our first real "nonflip" home. Things seemed to be getting downright comfortable as far as the Little Shop and the online store went. We also finally started selling the houses in the development we had built. The construction of these thirty-six single-family homes had almost bankrupted us over the previous couple of years, so getting them off our hands meant we could pay off some debts that felt like a noose around our necks.

At last Jo and I were sleeping well at night again. Our relationship was good, we had pretty much worked out the whirlwind of business growth, and we were figuring out how to juggle starring on a television show while raising four kids. All this was about all we could handle, but we were handling it. We were even seeing our financial numbers go into the black, and honestly things felt great. And wouldn't you know, the moment we finally had a little extra cash to stash away . . .

Jo had a vision.

It happened when she was dropping the kids off at school one day. For the first time she noticed—as in, really noticed—some abandoned buildings across the street capped off by two desolate, rusty old silos. It's amazing how something so large could have sat there right in the heart of downtown Waco without anyone in town paying them much notice. And if they did, they were no doubt hoping that some wealthy developer would sweep through and tear those rusty old things down. But that's the thing about Jo: she sees beauty in places where other people aren't even looking.

"Chip, just imagine if we put all of our businesses in that one spot. I could open a much bigger shop, and we could have our offices upstairs. The kids' school is right across the street, and I'd be able to see them on the playground from my office window. We could even walk over to have lunch with them."

Jo made an excellent argument. These were all valid points. She really delivered this thing with a bow on top.

When we drove by the place that first day and peered in through the chain-link fence, the excitement in Joanna's voice made me want to jump out of the car and grab that property for her right then and there. I felt a bit like the man wanting to lasso the moon for his sweetheart. The thing is, Jo had gotten behind every crazy dream I'd come up with over the years. Now *she* was the crazy dreamer. When she first started dreaming about opening Magnolia Market back in 2003, I had basically pushed her into it. But this time, it was Jo wanting to leap. And I was gonna do everything in my power to help her do it.

The price of the property itself wasn't completely out of reach, but developing it would be the biggest project we had taken on to date. It would cost us just about every penny we had to our name. But we'd grown accustomed to risking it all on just about every investment we'd done prior.

The financial risk was big on this property because of the sheer size of it. Just the grain barn alone was twenty thousand square feet. Not to mention the thousand-square-foot former floral boutique—which was, without a doubt, the most charming part of the property. Jo was already daydreaming about turning that building into a European-style bakery. And of course, the most striking feature of the property was the actual silos themselves. Those beautiful relics were massive—kind of like round exoskeletons of two high-rise buildings, each over a hundred feet tall. Each featured about four thousand square feet of potential usable space just waiting to be brought back to life. And because each silo was over a hundred feet tall, there was plenty of potential to add floors and expand the square footage even further.

The Silos property before renovation began.

There was just one problem. When we priced out what it would cost to do the renovations on all those old buildings, even the lowest estimates we received were in the millions of dollars.

I hate to break it to you, but landing a reality TV show does *not* make you a millionaire.

Clearly this was the riskiest thing we'd ever done by a mile. But Jo's instincts are sharp, and she wasn't wavering on this one.

Up until that point in our business relationship, Jo had always been the one who was risk averse. She shied away from the idea of overextending ourselves. I had always been the one pushing the envelope and willing to take a bigger risk for a bigger reward.

But I'd never heard her talk so passionately about a dream before. She sounded like *me*, but this time she was talking about a deal that could potentially put us millions—yes, I said *millions*—of dollars in debt.

I suddenly wondered if I'd created a monster. Typically the thrill of something like this would propel me forward, but this time I hesitated.

How do you make a decision like that—put everything on the line for one dream? There are no guarantees in life, and there sure as heck are no guarantees in television. We had no idea what the future held for the show. It could be over tomorrow. Our Magnolia clientele could disappear overnight. With the future uncertain, the thought of sinking everything into such a large property was completely terrifying.

Yes, it could be perfect . . . *if* our wildest dreams came true. But anything short of that would make this property embarrassingly excessive.

By the time you're reading this book, you may know how it all played out. But what you probably don't know is how we came to our decision . . .

Jo gets a pretty strong sense about where God is leading her, and until she feels a certain peace, she doesn't move. For me, though, it works a little differently. I've always believed in just going for it—making decisions, taking the risk, doing the work, whatever the work may be—knowing that God will be right there with me. If the thing I do turns out great, then I can rest easy, knowing I was probably on the right path. That's a win. If it turns into a disaster, well then, God somehow uses that for my good too. He teaches me something I couldn't have understood any other way. So I chalk that up to an even bigger gain.

For people with a winner mentality, there's a positive waiting for you no matter the outcome. For those with a loser mentality, if there's a negative outcome anywhere along the way, you perceive that you've lost. That's why I always say winning and losing isn't an event; it's a mind-set.

I think a lot of people tend to take every win and every loss as some sort of a play-by-play: if you win, you win, and if you lose, you lose. But

I don't see life like that at all. There's a much bigger game going on, and if you step back from the play-by-play and look at the big picture, the ability to make decisions gets a whole lot less daunting.

Think of it like tennis. You're Serena Williams. You're at Wimbledon. You win. You lose. You win. You win. You lose. You lose. (Serena Williams is a hero of mine. No way would she lose this much, but let's pretend.) This goes on set after set until the match is over. Winning the *match* is the goal. So after any win or loss, you adjust your strategy accordingly and press forward. Even if you're way down, you don't throw in the towel—at least not until the whole thing is over.

If you want to be a winner, then you have to prove yourself through all of the ups and downs over years and years of playing the game. *One match does not define a legacy.*

Our family went to the 2017 Super Bowl in Houston. The game we witnessed that day was between the New England Patriots and the Atlanta Falcons, and it was one for the history books.

I'm a southern boy, and while I'm not going to go on and on about the New England Patriots, even us Texans have to give credit where credit is due: quarterback Tom Brady and his teammates never gave up. Not for one second.

The announcers were calling it for the Falcons before the third quarter was even over. The Falcons had this thing so far in the bag that all sorts of people who paid who-knows-how-much money for their seats left the stadium early just so they could beat the traffic. Patriots fans, who are known as some of the most die-hard fans of any game anywhere, started turning off their TVs before the game was over.

But Brady and his band of cohorts? Uh-uh. No way. They kept their heads in the game. They never stopped trying to win.

And against all odds, those Patriots started to turn it around.

One play after another—*boom!*

It looked and felt like a major comeback, and the Patriots fans at Houston's NRG stadium started cheering as if the impossible might actually happen. They were still eight points down, and Brady got sacked.

I thought to myself, *Well, that's the ball game, but they did give it a good college try.*

Then the very next thing I saw was Tom Brady doing what only Tom Brady can do.

He twisted free.

He launched a pass.

Then they made a touchdown.

Then a two-point conversion.

And all of a sudden the game was tied!

If you can believe it, the game was now in overtime—the very first overtime of any Super Bowl. Ever. And get this: the Patriots eventually won it. From twenty-five points down, they won!

It was the greatest comeback in Super Bowl history.

And my point here is this: If you looked at that game play by play over the course of the night, the Patriots looked like they were going to lose. Again and again and again, they "lost." But Tom Brady and Coach Bill Belichick and the rest of the team never saw it that way. That wasn't their mind-set. If they saw themselves as losers based on their play-by-play reality, then that game really would have been over before they even got to the fourth quarter. They would have just gone through the motions and finished out on the losing side of history. But they didn't.

Those dudes didn't even consider losing as a possibility. Against million-to-one odds in Vegas, they bet on themselves.

Not only did they win, they made history.

Listen to me here: if you're going to make a bet, bet on yourself. Of course you won't always win. Life doesn't work that way. But if you don't at least try, how could you ever know what's on the other side?

A long time ago Jo and I built a foundation of betting on ourselves, and we weren't about to stop just because the stakes got higher. Suddenly, with the silos, we were faced with putting our money where our mouths were. This was our moment. So, with a good dose of fear and trembling, once again we bet on ourselves.

In hindsight, of course, our decision was a good one, and we ended up looking pretty smart. The renovations took way longer and cost far more money than we'd budgeted and also caused far more stress than our show was able to capture on television. But Magnolia Market at the Silos was a massive hit from day one. What Jo saw in her mind that day, as we peered through the chain-link fence, is the very thing people now come from all over to experience.

We both know this could have turned out much differently. This whole thing could've gone bust and been a gigantic financial mess. And yet I'm confident Jo and I would've found our way through it. We might have landed on our sorry broke butts, and we may have had to take a moment to lick our wounds, but we would've helped each other back up and eventually gone on to chase another dream.

That's just what we do: Gaineses never quit. We look at the long game and consider the final score. And even when the decks are stacked against us, we keep on betting on us.

CHAPTER 10

WACKO, TEXAS

For a long time it seemed like our hometown existed in the shadows of a dark storm cloud. Most people who even knew our town existed thought of it as a backwater, a place where nothing happened—unless it was something awful like the Branch Davidian disaster back in 1993. (Which, by the way, didn't happen in the actual city of Waco . . . but that's another story.)

Back in college, I knew a lot of people who wouldn't even own up to living here. They would say that they were from "Central Texas," a term that blankets a good stretch of this area, all the way down to Austin. I myself was guilty of claiming I was from Dallas-Fort Worth because, although not currently accurate, it *is* where I grew up.

People typically reacted to the news of my being from Waco with sympathy or disdain. After the Branch Davidian incident, the name of our town even became part of popular culture. It was routinely called out in movies, on television shows, in songs, and by late-night comedians in the worst ways possible.

But none of that deterred Jo and me when we chose to cast our lot with Waco. Actually, it did just the opposite, because it seems that some of us are hardwired with a strong urge to root for the underdog.

Just for fun, let's call us the underdoggers. We're the ones who see a strong, capable, powerhouse of an opponent and immediately feel compelled to root for the other side. This happens to us in sports, when we participate in politics, and of course during our favorite movies, where the nerdy kid ends up with the prettiest girl in school.

Sometimes the opponent is one lone giant, and other times it feels like the whole freakin' world. Either way, we underdoggers love to see the unexpected prevail. We get more joy out of the hard-fought, unforeseen successes than we ever could from the ones that everyone saw coming. (By the same token, we experience more pain from an unexpected failure than we do from the expected ones.) This is what gives us underdoggers that thrill in the first place.

In other words, if you're rooting for the long shot, you have much less to lose if they lose and a lot more to gain if they win. It's just simple risk versus reward.

I am a real estate guy, so I understand the importance of location. And Waco, of all places, is where Jo and I decided to put down our roots. Actually one of the things that initially drew Jo and me to each other was our shared desire to stay put in this town. It makes me smile that one of our first all-in decisions together was betting on an underdog.

This was also the first time Jo and I noticed our shared ability to see the beauty in the rubble. We have since made a life out of expecting and working toward restoration at every turn. Establishing our roots here in this city was us declaring what team we were going to fight for—for the long haul.

We bet on Waco. No matter the outcome, no matter what the cost.

To us, restoration can be about a home, a marriage, a family, or anything looking for a new story. For the better part of fifteen years, Magnolia Homes has been remodeling houses under the tagline "Making Waco Beautiful One Home at a Time." Even back when we started, we knew that one home being restored makes a real difference, just as investing in one person makes a real difference.

I am not going to get into the details of Waco's history. This is not an attempt to gloss over the bad stuff or to pretend it didn't happen. This is our history, and our city owns that. At the same time, more than ample attention has been given to the city's negative past. I don't want to pay tribute to it by lingering on it for even another minute. It's time to look ahead, not behind, to focus on the future, on full restoration.

In my opinion, this town was built for such a time as this.

I'm not the only one who thinks that way either. For years, people and churches of all different denominations and belief systems around Waco have been coming together to pray over and to believe for the restoration of this city. They've been expectant for something big and powerful to take place to reenergize our hometown. And something big is happening.

This is a resilient underdog of a town, and it just needed a chance.

LOCATION, LOCATION, LOCATION

In the world of real estate, one factor reigns supreme. Real-estate agents know that if you have the right location, the rest of the equation will come together. The details on your wish list can be replicated or added. However, if the place is in a less-than-desirable area of town, they will remind you of the severe risks you are taking. Depending on whether or not we're discussing a residential or commercial property, location can affect resale, safety, schools, traffic, culture or lack thereof, status, walkability, pollution, local politics, property taxes and value, quality of life, area attractions, and on and on.

There are endless factors that go into determining whether this particular piece of real estate is in a great location or if it's in a place where you can't even give the thing away. For a long time Waco was the latter. Homes and land were dirt cheap, well below the national average. Waco, in general, was not considered a good investment.

And yet this is the place Joanna and I call home. It's the city where I opened my first small business, and it's where Jo and I wanted to base Magnolia.

In hindsight, of course, we wouldn't have it any other way. I even have to laugh about the specific locations we've hitched our wagon to within the city limits. We have consistently chosen some of the most questionable parts of town to set up shop. (Maybe our underdogger impulses got the best of us.)

Jo's original Magnolia Market, for instance, was located in an old house in a transitional area of town with no other similar retail nearby. When driving past, most people wouldn't even have noticed the shop if they weren't looking for it. Not because the place wasn't cute—it was. It's just because that particular area wasn't necessarily the go-to spot in town to shop for home decor. Anyone coming there was more likely looking for used washer and dryer parts or a mom-and-pop hardware shop. But still, somehow, it worked.

Another example of this disregard for location is the housing sub-division Jo and I built. It's located less than a mile from the Little Shop on Bosque. Where some people may have seen few opportunities or even neglect in the area, we saw possibilities. So, we built this darling little development smack dab in the middle of an area we thought was ready for a renewal.

Then, years later, we chose some rusty old silos in one of the most un-sought-after portions of downtown. In the 1940s and early 1950s, this area was actually bustling and booming, and the site would've been prime real estate. But that was before an F5 tornado rolled through downtown and tore everything apart. The entire area never quite bounced back. On top of that, the silos were located right by the train tracks. Every few hours a freight train would roll through, blasting its horn all the way past. It still does. The people who are sitting on the Magnolia Market lawn relaxing, enjoying a beautiful day at the Silos, are suddenly scared out of their minds before they realize it is in fact *not* a meteor falling out of the sky.

These are the types of things that normal folks would notice during an initial real-estate tour and simply say, "Thanks, but no thanks." These are the types of things that in some cases make a property unsellable. But to us, the quirky features and charm we saw on those sites were just what we were looking for.

Considering Waco's reputation and relatively small size, it was hard to convince HGTV to believe that basing our show solely in Waco, Texas, would be a recipe for success. Even folks in Waco kept asking us, "How are you ever going to find enough houses?" The network tried to talk us into doing just the first few homes in Waco and then branching out into neighboring cities like Austin or Dallas. We completely understood their perspective. But we felt we had to hold firm on this because our family was here and our kids were young. Not to mention that our business was based in Waco, and it would be hard to travel such long distances and still maintain the quality we'd grown to expect from ourselves. After some discussion the network understood that if they wanted us, a show based in Waco, Texas, had to be enough for them.

Then a miracle happened: HGTV got excited about the city being featured as part of the background of our new show. They started showing the most beautiful elements of this special town. They captured gorgeous sunrises, amazing sunsets, windmills, the farm, the shop, the warehouse, downtown Waco, historic Austin Avenue, Baylor University, the two rivers (the Brazos and the Bosque) that meet just north of downtown—anything that was special about this town, they highlighted it. And this publicity started evolving into an incredible opportunity for the city.

I guess what I'm saying is that Waco turned out to be our muse, and we found the experience to be mutually beneficial. Our loyalty to our family and this town could've ended this show before it even started. But as it turned out, God had a different plan for us all.

If you want to talk about history, or a town's reputation, check this out. Up until the early 1900s, Waco was known for its healing waters. There was an artesian well that allegedly had medicinal benefits for those with illnesses or diseases. Those who soaked in that water for ten minutes or longer claimed to experience healing benefits. The way the story goes, people would enter with crutches and leave the waters no longer needing them. This phenomenon drew lots of people into our little city. Then for some reason, over time, those waters dried up.

Now here we are, years later, and somehow this show and the renaissance happening here in Waco is giving people that same refreshing and inspired feeling that nineteenth-century folk once traveled such long distances to experience.

So yeah, we took a chance on this town. That's what you do when you love something. You don't excuse or ignore it. You don't tuck it away. You bring it into the light, no matter what anyone else might think.

Jo and I bet on Waco, and Waco bet right back on us.

This town was already chock-full of amazing people before we even arrived. Its streets were (and still are) sprinkled with quirky, hidden gems—unique, local places just waiting to be discovered. Waco was primed for an awakening. It had had this beautiful fire in its belly for years, and it only took a few sparks to see this thing ignite.

The relatively small size of the city is an asset as well. In Waco, if you do something fun or creative, it is the talk of the town. Paint a mural on the side of a random building? The next day approximately 3,047 Wacoans will have tweeted or Instagrammed a selfie in front of said mural. Paint that same mural in San Francisco or Nashville? *Maybe* a random dog will pee on it. But in a place like this, every small pebble dropped has major ripple effects. Small things can have a massive impact. And suddenly the little city that was so easily overlooked starts to catch your attention.

As they say, a rising tide lifts all boats. When the underdog starts to gain momentum, you can just feel that things are about to get exciting. And that's happening in Waco right now. It has become a place that people want to come visit from all over the country. People are actually moving here, and students graduating from local colleges are choosing to make Waco their permanent home at unprecedented levels. Realtor.com listed Waco as the most frequently searched city in the country.[1] Good things are happening, and when asked, I say, "Waco is the land of opportunity."

Over the last few years, Waco has changed more than I could fit in this book. Cool new places are popping up all over town. (Creativity breeds more creativity.) The fact that we have been able to play a part in this restoration story has been one of the greatest joys of our lives. We have teamed up with people who have fought for this city for decades and with those who are just now joining in. Together, we are rewriting Waco's history. The old has gone, the new has come, and the future couldn't be more beautiful.

These days we see between thirty and forty thousand visitors a week at the Silos. And you and I both know these folks aren't driving all the way across the country because they need some home decor items stat. We hear stories every week about people who have chosen to visit for a whole slew of reasons—birthdays and anniversaries, honeymoons, and bucket lists. We are humbled and honored by the number of terminally ill people who have chosen Waco as the destination of their last trip. Though those healing waters may have dried up more than a hundred years ago, there is some sense of peace or refreshment that seems to be drawing people here still. There is something deeper going on in our city, and it's pretty remarkable to witness.

I believe with all my heart that this town was built for times like these. Waco has already experienced one "Miracle on the Brazos" (a big football win in the 1970s), and it sure feels like a second one is in the making. We've only just begun on the full restoration of this town. There is still so much work to be done. While by many standards we're still an underdog, we won't grow complacent. We've got a lot of fight left in us yet.

CHAPTER 11

SCRAPPY IS AS SCRAPPY DOES

If I had to describe myself in one word, it would be *handsome*. But if I had to pick another word, it would be *scrappy*.

I understand that for some, the word *scrappy* may have a negative connotation. Maybe you think of a school-aged kid, small for his age, but out there mixing it up with some of the bigger kids in the grade above just to get a reaction out of them. Or maybe you picture a bunch of young men on a basketball court, elbowing one another and taking cheap shots just to get some points on the board. It's even possible that it brings to mind the neighborhood stray cat that sneaks into your back-yard, knocks over the trash can, and eats last night's table scraps.

You picking up what I'm putting down? The knee-jerk reaction to the word *scrappy* is usually something along the lines of "do whatever it takes to get a leg up," no matter who you may hurt along the way.

Forget all that. That's not the way I understand the word at all. I take the word to mean: To have grit. To never give up. To be willing to take a guess even if you don't have all the information.

We use the word *scrappy* so often at Magnolia, and whether you perceive it in a humorous or endearing way, it's a rallying call for us here. To us it looks a whole lot different than elbowing and roughhousing. I found this definition on UrbanDictionary.com, and I like it: "Someone or something that appears dwarfed by a challenge, but more than compensates for seeming inadequacies through will, persistence and heart."[1]

These three attributes eclipse formal training, in my opinion, any day of the week. Without a doubt, we scrappy types will do whatever it takes when we're going head-to-head with challenges. When others bail for one reason or another, we're just getting warmed up. To me that's what it means to be scrappy.

I'm not sure how we all came to have these qualities at Magnolia, but one way or another, we all seem to have drunk the Kool-Aid. At least 75 percent of our workforce are millennials, and for a lot of them, this is their first real job. I'm forty-two and almost twice the age of the average employee at our company, so I still have a couple of things to teach these kids. But it's always been my style to let people figure things out on their own, and there's something inherently scrappy about that.

You may not know this (and even if you do, you'll likely not remember it), but you only retain 5 percent of the content you learn through a lecture unless you pretty quickly go out and either put that content to use or teach someone else what you've just learned. If you do that, you will likely remember most of it—like 90 percent.[2] That's because when we teach or implement new knowledge immediately after hearing it, we retain it far better. Our brains work harder this way, and we are forced to reason through the logic. It causes us to focus and concentrate in order to solve problems, and this process reinforces what we've learned.

I'm a firm believer that figuring things out on your own is more effective than being given something on a silver platter. And that belief is at the heart of my personal leadership strategy. I expect our team to dive in headfirst. They don't have time to doggie-paddle. We pride ourselves in on-the-job training and solving problems. I like people who work first and ask questions later. As soon as I get a sense that they're sitting back in their comfort zone, avoiding a challenge, I push them off the ledge. That may sound harsh, but people who know my heart understand my intentions behind this. I've got a different take on the whole concept of sink or swim. In my opinion, you win either way. If you swim, that means you're capable. If you sink, that simply means you need more practice. It's less of an "if you don't make it, you aren't good enough" mind-set and more of an opportunity to truly assess where you are and what you still need to work on.

⅄

For a long time, it was just me and the guys—Shorty, Melesio, and Jose—who worked on all of our renovation projects. But then we hired Kristen to help out with overall project management. She poured her life into our business. I remember noting the hours she spent working alongside us. The boys and I would be doing hard manual labor, and yet I never questioned whether Kristen was pulling the exact same amount of weight.

When she first started, Kristen didn't go through any type of formal job training. She stepped into a world unknown and figured out how to get right to work. She's the type of team member who thrives at Magnolia. We've had employees who required a lot of hand holding and clarification, and those personality types have rarely been able to grow with us. For one reason or another, we end up going our separate ways.

Just about a month after she came on board, I presented Kristen with her first opportunity to take the lead on one of our remodel projects. Right before she got started, I sort of mentioned in passing not to forget to pull a permit. Sounds easy enough for anyone in the construction business, but I was pretty sure she'd have no clue what I was talking about. So she asked a perfectly normal question for someone who'd never done this type of work before: "How do I pull a permit?" I gave her a couple of suggestions to get her started and told her she needed to figure it out.

This is how people actually learn, folks. If I'd told Kristen exactly how to do it, she would have remembered that information for a day. But if she actively participated and figured things out on her own, I knew she'd remember it for a lifetime. I believe this approach pays some hefty dividends—for example, having a bunch of capable employees instead of a bunch of babies.

And here's what happened. Kristen called around until she figured out which office she needed to go to. Then she marched herself down to the city offices and asked questions until she was blue in the face. And then she finally, *finally* pulled her first permit. What would've taken somebody with some experience an hour took Kristen the better part of a day. But she'd made it past step one of the permit-pulling process. Check.

Sweet Kristen had this job almost across the finish line when the inspector called to set up the electrical inspection. Pro tip: If there's work being done inside a wall (such as electrical), then the inspection has to take place *before* you close up the framing with drywall or shiplap or whatever material you are using to enclose the walls or ceilings. But how would you know that if you're new to the job and no one ever told you? So she had to rewind and open the wall back down to the studs.

Kristen will tell you today that she could not have been more frustrated with me throughout that entire project. She'd point out that I knew exactly who to call and what to do. And she's exactly right. I did. But she'll also tell you that her "baptism by fire" into the world of construction made her tough. She learned fast. And by being forced to figure it out, she not only gained our trust, but she also earned buy-in with both the contractors and the city. She gained authority by earning it herself, doing the work rather than by my offering it to her as a proxy.

From my perspective, the point was never to set her up for failure. I'm not one to intentionally hamstring anyone. But I would've much rather she tried and failed than be given the guidebook and never learned how to really figure things out on her own. The reality is, that mistake cost *me*. But I'm willing to invest in paying twice to have walls closed up if the return is growth for my team.

Kristen is just one (exceptional) example of many talented, scrappy employees who learned to dive in and swim on their own at Magnolia. And the fact that our whole team has adopted this way of thinking gives Magnolia a competitive edge.

When Jo and I reopened Magnolia Market back in May 2014, we decided that we wanted to establish a culture that challenges and stretches our employees past what they *think* they can do straight into their "discomfort zone." We weren't interested in hiring people who were looking for a fancy job title and a cushy desk job. There's nothing wrong with that; it just wasn't our way. We specifically looked for people who seemed ready and willing to take on the task at hand, no matter what that meant.

U N - S U M - U P - A B L E

A RABBIT TRAIL

For the record, job titles really bug me. They feel like some sort of pat on the back or a symbol of self-importance. I've never had a title, and hope I never do. I'm not even sure what my business card would say. Chip Gaines, Builder? Goat Wrangler? I don't think someone's value can be bottled up into a job title. I've fought this for a long time.

Early on, it was hard to give our team members titles because each one was responsible for so many different tasks that their work couldn't have been summed up in two or three words. And I liked it that way just fine. Eventually

---

I gave in, simply because the lack of titles was causing a lot of internal and external confusion.

But my point here is, if you want to do well in your work, don't get caught up in the job-title mentality. Let your work speak for itself rather than relying on some title that someone else gave you or confining yourself to a simple job description.

It's just so easy to let that title box you in. If you're low man on the totem pole and your title hints at that, then you may put yourself in that box rather than think of ways to go above and beyond, exceeding every expectation. On the other hand, if you're a head honcho with a big title, then you're likely to rest on it. You may settle in and get comfortable. And that's exactly what you *don't* want if you really want to grow professionally. I should also make mention that never becoming complacent with your position is the best way to make yourself invaluable to whoever you work for. Make yourself irreplaceable to your company, and you will have your choice of titles that can't define you.

Being a young business plays into our shoot-from-the-hip, do-whatever-it-takes mentality. But even more than that, we're always innovating and continually looking for new ways to serve our customers.

This learn-as-you-go mind-set has given our team a competitive advantage that allows us to take on challenges with fresh eyes and sharp instincts. We've looked, but there haven't been many experts on what we've jokingly deemed the "Seven Rs of Global Domination" (Retail, Renovation, Rentals, Real Estate, Ranching, Restaurant, and Reality Show) knocking down our doors to offer any sage advice. We have been forced to figure this stuff out the old-fashioned way. As a result, the lessons we've learned reside not only in our heads but in our hearts. And as my girl Kristen will testify, they've changed our lives forever.

Some may think that learning as you go sounds like amateur hour, but *au contraire, mon frère.** Because we didn't learn what *won't* work, we've found that nothing is impossible.

The very landscape of our business has changed drastically over the years, and nothing has come without sacrifice and hard work. It's taken a lot of people a lot of long hours to get all seven Rs up and running. There are a handful of folks who have been with us since we first reopened the shop, and most sane people probably would've jumped ship by now. Maybe that's saying something about Magnolia, but honestly I think it's really saying something about these individuals. They've seen us through all kinds of growing pains, and in the spirit of scrappy, we love to look back now and count the number of drastically different positions some of these folks have held.

Our founding team members, you see, didn't just pick one responsibility; they picked four or five. Every day they showed up, wore multiple hats, and did the work of a whole team all by themselves. Whatever was needed, they jumped in and made it happen. In retrospect, even if we'd had a ton of money and could do it all over again, I wouldn't have chosen to hire a different crew to build this company with.

Our people may have lacked experience and, looking back, that was risky, but one thing our people didn't lack was talent. If there was a problem, they solved it, and only true talent can consistently create these types of results. But even more important is the fact that each one of our employees really bought in to the spirit of our organization. They carried—and carry!—our vision in their hearts as fiercely as Jo and I do.

---

* I haven't been to France, but Google translator says this means "on the contrary, my brother."

That's something that would baffle even the most seasoned headhunter. They've grown up with us, and they've helped the company grow up too.

Our people enjoy the process, and they refuse to let things fall through the cracks. If there is a hole, they are going to fill it even if they are already doing their fair share. For example, our top executives will be found wearing "Staff" T-shirts on a really busy weekend or helping pack boxes when the warehouse gets slammed. It doesn't matter how the job description reads; at Magnolia, it's all hands on deck.

The people within our organization carry this rare passion and buy-in, and Jo and I don't take it for granted, because you can't teach passion. No salary can draw it out of someone. It's either there or it's not. It's a fire in the belly.

I'd go to war any day with this group we've assembled here at Magnolia. That's the way I feel about this team. I'm well aware of the impact each one has on the bigger picture. As the "general" of this company, I'm not blind to the fact that without these good, hardworking people packing boxes in our warehouse or hammering away on our job sites, none of this would even be possible. When it's all said and done, they are the people whose will, persistence, and heart give us the best chance of being successful.

When something seems insurmountable to most, we shrug, because we eat "insurmountable" for breakfast.

PART 3

A TIME TO BUILD

CHAPTER 12

NEVER QUIT YOUR DAY DREAM

You have to be smart to be funny. It's true. There have been actual studies conducted that prove funny people have higher IQs.[1] But there are a lot of different types of funny. And honestly, for the punch line to work, it's got to be authentic.

Funny in real life is pretty different from funny on TV. As life often works, when I'm being my naturally hilarious self, the cameras are rarely rolling. Or if they are, the lighting isn't right or a train is making a racket somewhere in the distance. So the producers ask me to do it over so they can get the best shot. As you can imagine, it's easy for "naturally funny" to get lost somewhere between the third and fourth try. And that's exhausting for me. I love to laugh. I love to joke and prank and be silly to the point of being obnoxious. But doing these things on command for the cameras is another thing entirely.

Now, you're probably thinking, *Wah! Poor little Chippy. Life is so hard for him. Being funny makes him feel tired.*

I've hesitated to mention this sooner for this very reason. Life isn't particularly hard for me; it never has been. I've had my challenges, but times are not tough. So who the heck am I to be complaining? But bear with me for a bit so I can make this excellent point: having to be funny on command feels a whole lot like having a boss. And having a boss is an entrepreneur's nemesis.

Lots of people don't want all of the pressure that comes with owning their own business. It feels like too much of a risk, and they are content to work for the system just so they can clock out at the end of the day. I'm the opposite. I like to work for myself, and I've been doing that since my very first lawn business. I'm happy to shoulder all the responsibility and cost if it means not having to answer to someone else.

So what I didn't think through when we signed up for a TV show was that I was really signing up for someone to manage my schedule and basically my whole life. Every day that we're shooting, I'm told where to be and when to be there and what shirt I should wear. I'm being bossed for the very first time in my adult life. And who I am runs perpendicular with the reality of having a "supervisor" and a nine-to-five schedule.

My season-five beard is a perfect case in point.* During our break between seasons, I started growing it out just for fun—basically to see if I could. I've had a few substantial five o'clock shadows in the past, but at this point in my life I was still a beard virgin. When filming started back up, I made the mistake of not shaving my beard and was informed pretty quickly that having the beard on the first day meant I had to keep it until the end of the season for continuity's sake.

So you can see how complicated this has gotten.

It started out pretty simple: "Hey! I'm going to grow my beard out to change things up for a couple of months."

Then it was: "Chip, you have to keep that beard for nine more months."

So now here I am with a beard on the cover of this book. Not exactly the look I was going for on the glossy sleeve of my juicy tell-all.

---

* And calm down, everybody. I hear your feedback loud and clear. Trust me; however much you hate the beard, I hate it more.

I have spent summers pounding the pavement, selling books door to door. I've trimmed trees and mowed acres of grass from dawn to dusk in the hot Texas sun—though not as hot as selling fireworks from a plywood stand during a roasting southern July. I've built retaining walls that held up entire hillsides from nothing and constructed new homes from scratch. I have come home at the end of the day weighing less than when I left in the morning, just from the copious amounts of water weight I'd lost through sweating. Perspiration and aching muscles don't bother me a bit. In fact, if I haven't worn myself out by the end of the day, if I don't come home with bruises or scratches, then I don't feel right. I feel unsettled, like I've shorted myself somehow. But when I've physically worked hard, it feels like a day well spent, and I've loved every minute of it.

But even after all of that manual labor, making a TV show is the most exhausting job I've ever done. And the reality is, it's not grueling work, at least not physically. It's also not rocket science, and it shouldn't drain me to the extent that it does. The irony is that on camera it appears that I'm just goofing off, playing really, when in reality it's the hardest work I do.

I feel enormous amounts of guilt for 'fessing up to all of this, because no matter how emotionally taxing this show can be, it has still been the opportunity of a lifetime for Jo and me. Every day we are grateful. *Fixer Upper* has allowed us to pursue so many dreams, so many things that we are truly passionate about. I never want to lose sight of that, even for a moment. But that doesn't mean it's always easy or natural for me to do the show.

And Jo loves it, by the way. She's a natural. She has no problem sticking with the schedule, and when the cameras start rolling, she is truly mesmerizing to watch. Some people are just made for the camera. I love to be on set and watch her come alive in her element. It's one of my favorite things to do—unless you include the times when I get to just come in and mess with her while she's working. Now *that* I really enjoy!

But the truth is, I am a builder and a contractor. I don't just play one on TV. I love nothing more than being with my team and making good progress out on a job site. And our filming schedule can be pretty disruptive to both the workflow of our construction business and my natural work rhythms.

Jo and I show up at a project ready to roll up our sleeves and get after it. And right as we get acclimated to what house we're working on and all of the nuances and specific plans and design details associated with it, we're tapped on the shoulder and notified that it's time to move on to get the next shot. That's just how television works.

On top of that is the enormous workload the show generates. We renovate around seventeen homes per season, each of which is filmed within a nine-month time span. And that's just the television portion of our construction business—off the air, we're almost always doing interesting projects in addition. Now, in real life, if you were to hire a contractor and team to come in and do any one of these projects, that alone could take up to nine months to complete. So you can only imagine the amount of jumping around Jo and I do in order to keep tabs on things.

Most people in the TV industry probably sought out a career in showbiz. They were formally trained or at least did theater in high school or college, then they auditioned for the parts they wanted. But Jo and I kind of fell into this TV thing by accident.

"Hey guys, want a TV show?"

"All right."

Maybe that's why audiences resonate with us. We don't seem so slick—because we're not. We don't use a hair and makeup or wardrobe team like most of our counterparts on TV. Jo puts on blush and eye makeup and such in the parking lot before we hop out to film. And as for me? You can just forget it. No makeup. No skinny jeans. No sandals. Just the same clothes I was wearing before we got into all this. So in a sense, what you see of me on *Fixer Upper* is what you get. But being a TV personality has never been my dream, my true passion, or what I consider to be my life's work.

We were created to live passionately—all of us, no matter our personality type or circumstance. The human heart was made to swell and jump and stir; that's a fact. It took me a while to figure out what makes my heart feel that way. But that is perhaps one of the most crucial things to know about ourselves.

Λ

What makes you want to jump out of bed in the morning? What puts a smile on your face, the kind you can't wipe off if you tried? What fascinates you? Motivates you? Overwhelms you in the very best sense? If you don't know, I suggest not wasting one more single day until you find out.

Here's what it looks like for me.

So far as work goes, my favorite part of all of it is the working part. I mean actual physical labor, the kind that makes you tired and sweaty. Getting up at four in the morning to tend the farm while the world is quiet—feeding animals, mucking stalls, gathering eggs, filling water troughs, checking fences, letting animals out into the field—is a high point to my day. Maybe it's because I'm task oriented and like seeing something through from start to finish. Maybe I just love the outdoors. I can't be sure what it is about this kind of work I love, but I know I love it.

It probably would be wiser, from a time-management standpoint, if I hired a crew to take care of the farm so I could get a little more rest. But the thing is, when I start my morning out there, I'm more productive for the rest of the day. That's God's own truth. Maybe it's because my farm chores guarantee that every day I have those two hours to myself. No texts or e-mails or phone calls or meetings. No producers sending me pictures of the shirt I'm supposed to be wearing.

Though farm chores and construction work are the most physically demanding labor that I currently do, they feel like recess to me. And there's something really beautiful about work that feels like play.

The way I see it, there's work and then there's *work*. And there's a big difference between your work and your job.

A *job* is a task done for an agreed-upon price, and *work* is the effort directed toward accomplishing a goal. See what I mean? A *job* is something you do for money. Your life's *work* is done for a bigger purpose, to fulfill a calling or a dream. And when you manage to find that work—that's when it starts feeling like play.

I want that for you and for me too. Don't allow yourself to get stuck grinding away on the job piece and lose sight of the work piece, the one that truly matters. There's nothing admirable or respectable about laying yourself down, day in and day out, for a job you hate—not if you have a choice.

Maybe you can't up and quit the job you hate. I understand that there are extenuating circumstances that can prevent you from being able to take that leap. But if you are sticking it out because of fear or passivity, there's nothing heroic about that. Do work that matters . . . to *you*.

Now, if you're like most people, you're somewhere in the middle. What you're doing to support yourself may not be the thing you feel like you were born to do, but it's not total drudgery either. I get that you might not love *every* part of your job. I don't think anyone does. As I've said, I don't love every aspect of running Magnolia or doing *Fixer Upper*. But I know from experience that if you can get to a place where you at least feel passionate about *some* of the work, the job part will become a lot more bearable.

Vocation is a powerful thing. Don't let it just happen to you. Chase after it, even if right now "chasing" feels a lot like limping. You're going to spend approximately ninety-two thousand hours of your life working, so figure out what drives you and run, don't walk, in the direction of making real, fulfilling work out of that dream. And even if that's not feasible right now, carve out a chunk of your day, week, and life for the things that fill you up.

Perhaps you can't quit your day job, and I understand that.

But never, ever quit your day dream.

CHAPTER 13

SEASON FINALE

When left to our own devices, Jo and I will literally work ourselves to death.

Even before we knew each other, we each had unusually high capacities for work, but together, they've grown exponentially. People ask us every day, "How the heck do you two do it all?" And we just kind of stare at each other and shrug our shoulders.

It obviously doesn't have anything to do with our self-care habits because, for the most part, our self-care habits are terrible. Jo and I don't eat right, we don't exercise, and we're awful at getting a good night's rest. Basically all we need to do is take up smoking to be the go-to guides for what *not* to do. Or the proof may be in the pudding, and our lifestyle is, in fact, the thing that's responsible for our capacity.

But while we Gaineses may be workhorses, we're also pretty clear on what our limitations are. Joanna and I have concluded that we can only do two things *really* well at one time. And I'm not talking about the rubbing-your-stomach-while-simultaneously-patting-your-head kind of multitasking. I'm talking about the big things. For example, it would not be wise for either of us to run for public office while researching molecular disintegration while *also* writing a screenplay for an epic docudrama, all while raising a young family. You know? That would not be smart for us. That would be our version of spreading ourselves too thin.

It's not that we *can't* juggle more than two things at a time. In fact, by definition there must be at least three things in play to call it juggling. And we're definitely capable of doing it. We just don't do it well. Something's eventually gotta give.

And to be honest, we're just about to that point.

Presently, three big things absorb my thoughts and my time. These major responsibilities affect my ability to sleep, and they steal from my peace of mind. Each is important. Each is worthwhile. And each is something that can't succeed without Joanna's and my personal involvement. Here they are in real time.

1. We're strengthening our marriage every day, which takes real time and effort, and we're raising four great kids who we couldn't be prouder of.
2. We are running a midsized business with multiple components called Magnolia.
3. We are filming a hot cable TV show about the ups and downs of designing and renovating homes.

The reality is that we can't afford to neglect a single one of these commitments. They're all opportunities of a lifetime, and none of them deserves our second best. And each feels like a huge responsibility with far-reaching implications.

Number one, our marriage and family, is by far the most important. There's not even a close second. This is our nonnegotiable. No one else in the world can raise our babies, and no one can better love and support my wife. No matter how successful I may have been at priorities two through a hundred in my life, if at the end of the day I didn't get number one right, I've failed.

Number two is our work. We've committed ourselves to our Magnolia business and employees. And as a young company, it needs our direct involvement. It's going to mature—we're hiring the right people, building great teams, and getting the right infrastructure in place—but it's simply too early to take ourselves out of the equation.

I dream of the day when Jo and I are chairmen of the board and not actually involved in the day-to-day operations, when our team will come to us only with high-level concerns, looking for counsel and direction. But the reality is, that day is in the future. For now, Magnolia still needs our vision, our leadership, and our day-to-day presence.

As for number three, the bottom line is there's just not anyone handsome and rugged enough to be my stand-in, and there's certainly no one hot enough to replace Jo. So you guessed it, only we can do this job too.

These past several years have been such a mind-blowing season of blessing for us. They have also been a very real struggle. I've been in this lengthy internal wrestling match, trying to understand and prioritize these three main priorities while also fending off all the other big things that compete for my time. Who deserves the best of me? Which ones get the bulk of my passion and energy? And which, in turn, gets what amounts to my leftovers?

In the beginning, of course, we could handle all three because everything was still pretty small. The shop had just opened back up, the show was just getting started, nobody really knew our names or faces yet, and we honestly didn't even know whether it was going to take off anyway. Even the babies were small back then.

However, before we knew it, the show became a huge success and undoubtedly gave our business a major lift, which we are so thankful for. We grew bigger and have been afforded more opportunities than we ever would have had without the show.

Success is such a complicated thing. All successful people want to be able to take at least some credit for their successes. But successful people also struggle in their heart of hearts about whether it was just luck, or just being in the right place at the right time, or something else.

Additionally, as a believer, I find myself wondering, *Why me? Why did God pick me of all people?*

And most of all, these days I find myself wondering, *What comes next?*

Are you familiar with Newton's cradle? It's that little desk toy with the row of metal balls all hanging from strings that hit each other from one end to the next when you pull one back and let it go. Actually, just see the diagram.

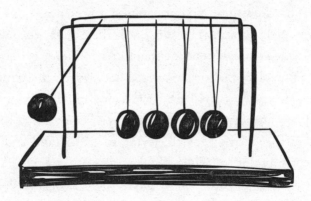

Newton's cradle is more than just a toy, actually. It demonstrates a principle of physics first described by Sir Isaac Newton in the seventeenth century—the law of conservation of momentum.[1] This law basically states that if something's moving at a uniform speed and direction, it will continue in that same motion until something comes and forces it to change direction.

I don't know if you've ever messed with one of these devices, but they are absolutely mesmerizing. Once those silver balls start swinging, they keep clicking away, back and forth for quite a while until something stops them, whether it's their own friction or someone's hand.

That toy reminds me of Jo and me. We will just go and go with no break unless something knocks us in another direction. In today's world, this tendency is sometimes viewed as a strength, but honestly, I'm not proud of it. In fact, I find it pretty unsettling.

We're currently shooting season five of *Fixer Upper* just as we have the previous four. We're in it, we're focused, we'd do this forever because—you know—momentum. For a long time, in the midst of the steady swing of marriage, babies, the business, and filming, Jo and I didn't really stop to take notice that we were just getting by rather than giving each one our very best. Against our better judgment, we told ourselves that "We've got it"—that we could, in fact, keep juggling our three priorities. That they weren't actually *that* big.

But guess what? We didn't actually have it.

It was really easy for us to feel like we could do it all when the show and the business were in the early stages. But the bigger things got—and they got big *fast*—the less energy we had to devote to all three. So much time was being allocated to filming that the details of the business were slipping. But it was easy for us to fall into the illusion that the business was doing just fine with a third of our attention because, after all, candle sales were still up.

Jo and I were going about our lives in our normal Newton's-cradle-like way until I was knocked off pace, into the opposite direction, by a tweet. And didn't we all know that a tweet would ultimately end life as we know it? I for sure had a sense of that.

THE TWEET THAT CHANGED EVERYTHING

I swear my tombstone will read "Death by Tweet." I am a serious Twitter aficionado. Want to make my day? Want to hurt my feelings? All you have to do is tweet at me. Those little 140-character messages can be like a hug or a dagger to the heart.

So I got this particular tweet at approximately two in the morning on a night when I was finding sleep particularly elusive. The tweet was from a customer who hadn't received an order.

Hey @chippergaines it's been 3 weeks, and I still haven't gotten my wreath. What's up?!

I wasn't happy about that, of course. But I tried to shake it off, knowing that I couldn't do anything about it then and that it would have to wait until morning. No luck. I was up all night dwelling on it. And Jo and I were scheduled to film at one of the projects we were working on the next morning, hair combed, by eight o'clock.

Midway through our second shot of the day, I started to get this weird, not-good, fuzzy feeling. I thought I must just be exhausted or dehydrated or something like that. I found a place to sit down and let my mind settle. But as I was sitting there, all of a sudden I was overwhelmed by a single thought.

What am I doing here?

A simple tweet about a late order from our online store was all it took for me to realize that I needed to recalibrate. I felt this overwhelming compulsion to walk off the set and head straight to our company's shipping warehouse. In my mind, I knew that I needed to be packing up orders and helping to get those packages out. We were behind on our ship dates, and this no longer felt like a distant problem that others were surely attending to. This was *my* problem, and I needed to be part of the solution. Who else but me should be figuring out what was ailing my growing business, and who else other than me should be ensuring that we moved beyond each and every one of these mistakes?

In the same instant it felt like Mexico all over again—like I was off chasing something trivial instead of taking care of my primary responsibilities. My construction company was a well-oiled machine; we had been doing what we do for nearly two decades now. But the retail side of our business was still just getting its feet under it, and it was suffering the consequences of my absence.

In that moment, something shifted within me. Suddenly filming the TV show looked like "the job" that had seduced me into giving it my precious time that I had always promised would be reserved for my true loves, my family and my business. How had this side gig found its way to competing with the very things that mean more to me than anything else in the world?

It's crazy how sometimes it takes something tiny to knock your steady pendulum swing into a completely different trajectory. That one symbolic tweet made me realize that although everything seemed to be going fine, the company really did need my daily leadership.

That tweet-fueled revelation also brought me to realize that Jo and I are tired. Don't take this to mean that we aren't doing well as a couple—that's definitely not the case. I'd even go as far as to say that we are doing better and are even more in love today than we have ever been. Joanna is my partner in family, business, and life in general, and that is never going to change. But pure long-term exhaustion can change a person—or two persons. We had been driving so hard for so long now. And I had this sense that if I kept my foot on the gas, we might be headed for disaster.

I have to admit that I'm already feeling it. Even the most menial tasks feel draining these days—and by this point in this book, you know that's not me. I know that Jo is worn out too. But she is naturally better at pressing on and often doesn't even realize how tired she is until she's crashed.

Have you guessed what I'm getting at? You probably have, but let me be direct. We haven't said the words out loud to many folks yet, but as I write them now they feel more real than ever:

We have decided to leave the show.

It's mile nineteen of this marathon we've been running, and I have hit the infamous wall. I can feel my body breaking down, and my mind is arguing with my heart, telling me that it's impossible to finish. (It's funny what your mind will tell you, and what you'll believe, when you are totally exhausted.)

But, the end of this race called *Fixer Upper* is drawing near. I can see the finish line off in the distance, and I do want to finish well. It's the only way I know to do it.

I learned a long time ago that if you ever consider quitting, it's already too late. When things get tough—and I mean really tough—you've already quit even if you don't know it yet. So we're not quitting the race in the middle. But we are looking ahead to the end of our run and wondering, then what?

It almost seems nonsensical to walk away from this miraculous gift from God, from the very thing that brought the world to our doorstep here in Waco, Texas. I understand that I've lapsed into new heights of melodrama, but I feel a bit like the biblical patriarch Abraham standing at his makeshift altar, arms around his precious son, facing the enormous sacrifice he believes he is being called to make.[2] *The Lord gives and the Lord takes away, and in all these things we're to bless him!*[3]

Obviously, leaving a television show behind is not in the same stratosphere as sacrificing one's son, and I'm certainly no Abraham. And yet I feel as though Joanna and I have gotten a small taste of that struggle. We have wrestled every which way with this decision, and still we end up on the same side:

It's time for us to lay it down.

Conventional wisdom would say that we are insane to even consider walking away now, and I'd be happy to list out the many reasons why this is true. I have every last one memorized as I turn them around and around in my head, usually in the middle of the night.

First of all, the show has been a hit. We are consistently one of the top shows in all of cable television—and trust me, nobody saw this coming. All of us have been completely amazed at *Fixer Upper*'s success.

Second, Fixer Upper *has been really, really good for our business.* Jo and I have always been business people. That's who we are. That's what we do. That's how we think. Our business has always been a central part of our story, and it was only natural for it to be a central part of the show. It was the fact that Joanna was actually a designer and I was legitimately a contractor that landed us the show in the first place. This authenticity seemed novel to the production company, and they pitched the show with that as the core concept. If Waco is a character on the show, then Magnolia definitely is too.

We didn't *start* our business to capitalize on the *Fixer Upper* audience, of course. As you now know, Magnolia's home-remodeling company preceded *Fixer Upper* by about thirteen years, and Jo had been selling home decor for a decade before the show first aired. But did the show grow these businesses? Absolutely. *Fixer Upper* is like a long, free infomercial about Magnolia every Tuesday night. So why would anyone walk away from a free advertising machine in the middle of establishing a new brand? Who in their right minds would give that up?

Third, and most important, we are about five hundred Magnolia employees strong at this point. That number typically shocks people, and that may be because we work hard at keeping this place feeling like a mom-and-pop shop. No matter how big our business might grow, we never want it to lose that feeling. And to me, these employees aren't just a number; they are the very lifeblood of this whole deal. Even though I don't know the name of every single person we employ like I used to, I carry each one of them. I feel an enormous amount of responsibility for them and their livelihoods. I think about their spouses and their children, about their health, their mortgages, their debts—and most of all, I think about their dreams and their futures.

We have built this amazing team of beautiful folks who show up each day and work their hearts out on our behalf. And in stepping away from the show, we are stepping into the unknown with all of them on our shoulders.

We have no idea what this all looks like once the screen goes dark.

In all of the wrestling that we did over whether or not we should stop doing *Fixer Upper*, the praying and seeking God, what really kept me up at night was wondering how leaving might affect all of *these people*, the people who risked going with us.

All this is to say that *yes*, we know we might be crazy to leave the show now. But we've been called crazy before. The decision to leave *Fixer Upper* has not been easy, and we are acutely aware of what the implications might be, but we still believe it's what we're to do.

We will forever be thankful to HGTV for taking a risk on us. Back when we began, that's what we were—a big risk, pretty far outside the box of the "talent" they usually hired. They have been good partners to us, and we will always be so proud of the beautiful thing we created together. HGTV has been an amazing place to learn the ins and outs of television. We have received the education of a lifetime, and we wouldn't trade that for the world.

HGTV also provided us with a platform to share our perspective, and we are grateful for that too. In an industry that doesn't often show authentically happy marriages, we have loved getting to go in front of the camera and laugh, hug, argue, collaborate, and cheer each other on. These are all the things we do with or without the cameras rolling. But getting to show people this version of marriage has truly been one of our favorite parts in all of this.

And sure, staying on the show for a few more years makes all the sense in the world. It's at the height of its popularity, breaking network and cable records, and we have a full spectrum of offers coming our way. A couple more years could make all the difference. But at every step of the way there'll be another ante, another all-in required of us. Who knows where it all would end?

It's easy to talk a big game when you have nothing on the line. It's a lot harder to put your money where your mouth is when it could cost you everything. And in a way, we've never had more at stake. This decision may severely affect our finances as well as our opportunities. What's ours for the taking right now may be expired when we come back around. If we leave now, there's no guarantee that anyone will be calling tomorrow.

Even so, there is only one way forward for us. And we're all right with that.

We probably don't see it the way the rest of the world does. If things stop selling, if the offers stop coming and our money dwindles away, I couldn't care less. Seriously. If you don't hear anything else, hear this—I don't care enough about my finances to compromise my family or their well-being. We've had empty pockets before, and that's nothing we can't take on again.

The education Jo and I have gotten through the process of making this decision has changed everything. What we knew going into this opportunity years ago made us a force to be reckoned with. But armed with what we know now, I feel like we are unstoppable.

And when the day comes when we can take a step back from Magnolia, there will still be many things we're excited to explore. There will be new challenges to conquer and new facets of society to disrupt. And there may even be a show or two in our future. Jo has always loved the medium of television, and maybe I'd love it more if I didn't feel like my hands were committed to raising my beautiful family and to building this amazing company.

For now, though, I'm committed to doing two things well—not three. Because in the end, if my family isn't at its best and my marriage at its absolute strongest, then I will move mountains to make those things right. Jo and I need a break. We have been running this marathon together that never seems to end, and we need to take some time, catch our breaths, and focus on our family and our business.

It's difficult to give your heart and soul to something that no longer inspires you, and for us, that's the show. It has been beautiful and wonderful, and our fifth, final season is our favorite yet, even if getting to the finish line has been a struggle. But I know for sure that we've left it all out on the field, every bit of love and care we have to give to those homes and these families—we gave it all away. We have no regrets and nothing left to give on that front.

There's no question that the show was a miracle. From the very beginning, we have seen the hands of God all over it. But we are confident that it was never meant to be the end goal for us but rather a means to an end. We are attempting to impart something important and meaningful on the earth far beyond simply home decor or home renovations. And the show has given us a powerful platform for these goals as well as enabling Magnolia to begin to do the beautiful things it was created to do. But closing the show does not mean we're going to stop moving toward those goals—or trusting God to show us what to do next.

The thing about walking closely with God is it has to be a minute-by-minute, day-by-day kind of relationship. No formula can suffice. You have to keep listening, keep following, keep being willing to act and to move on when it's time.

If you'll remember, the manna from heaven that God sent to sustain the people of Israel in the desert was only good for one day.[4] It was miraculous, but it also came with an expiration date. And so do many of God's blessings in this life. The fact that something is from God does not mean it's forever. The Lord gives, remember, and the Lord takes away.

One of the things I've learned about God in my forty-two years is that he loves to obliterate the boxes we put him in. There's no way to predict the way he speaks to us or leads us. In this case, he spoke to me through a tweet, and in an instant I knew our miracle had served its purpose. The lessons were learned. The blessings were distributed. It was time to let go of this beautiful experience called *Fixer Upper*.

God had given us this gift that I knew was ours to unwrap and enjoy. Even as we were being stretched by juggling those three priorities in our lives, he covered my family and our business. They are both doing well—so well in fact, I can only attribute their state to the miraculous. But if I were to continue on with the show now, I know that I would be taking things into my own hands.

God's grace lasts as long as it is required. But when the grace and peace start to go, it's a good time to evaluate if God is still in what you're doing. When I did just that, it became crazy clear to me that if I continued on, too scared to let my aging miracle go, I'd risk losing one of the two commitments that I have been tasked with taking care of for the long haul.

One is our business. Our ongoing prayer is that when people visit Magnolia in Waco, Texas, or even receive a package from us on their doorstep, they will be inspired to go love their own homes more—and behind that, to pour more love into their families and even their own lives. We really do want this company to be a vehicle of hope on earth.

And then of course, my one true desire is to love my beautiful wife and to raise our babies well. I want to give them each the best possible chance to make it. I want them full of courage and confidence and compassion. If I get this one right, I have nothing more to prove.

I have no clue what the future holds at this point. God surely has a few more surprises in store for us, yet I refuse to box him up. I refuse to limit what our story might look like in the months and years to come.

I can say no to everything the world offers. But any gift God has for me, I'm taking it.

=============

CHAPTER 14

TEAM OF RIVALS

In the mood for a parable?

Good.

Let's say I'm digging a ditch. The day is young, the sun is hot, and there's plenty of hole left to dig. And then some random guy walks past and offers to give me a hand.

What's my answer? It's yes. No pondering. No questions. Just yes.

In a situation like that, it seems crazy to stop to consider the potential helper's pastimes or belief systems. Say he practices homeopathic medicine or chases after tornados or believes in alien life-forms. What business is that of mine? I'm just thrilled to have an extra set of hands helping out. When you are busy getting real work done, being choosy about who you're willing to work alongside seems like a pretty big luxury to me.

Now, if we're in that ditch all day, there's bound to be some time to talk. So in the case of the storm chaser, I ask him to share his thoughts about inclement weather. And since we've got plenty of time, I take advantage of the opportunity to learn about what he does and why he is so passionate about it. I begin to understand a little of what makes him tick, and I even learn something of where he came from and where he's been.

There's a good chance that this tornado chaser (or maybe the alien-loving, homeopathic-practicing, amateur ditch digger) has something to say that I need to hear. I'm a pretty opinionated guy, but I try to just listen—and not the kind of listening where I wait for a lull in his monologue just so I can jump in and be heard. Instead, I try to really listen past the *what* to the *why*—because it's so hard to learn when I'm sure that I already know the answers.

Maybe this new acquaintance never gets around to asking about me, what I think about and believe in and the future that I hope for. He doesn't think to ask, or maybe he doesn't care to know. Then again, he may be genuinely interested in getting to know me after all. If he asks, I start with some of the easy stuff—the names and ages of my kids, the town I grew up in. But as the day goes on, eventually there's nowhere to go but straight to the matters of the heart.

Turns out, the ditch we're digging is the length of the divide between us, the span of our differences, and there's so far to go before sundown.

As we keep on digging, if he lets me, I eventually share what wakes me up in the night. The things that make my head a bit dizzy because I love them so much, and the horrible, awful stuff that makes my blood run cold. I'm a talker and could go on and on about these things for some time, but I hold back. This gentleman has already been so selfless in laboring beside me, I don't need to talk his ear off.

When I picture this event in my mind's eye, we look pretty different. Different height, different hair and eye color, even different skin tones. When he speaks, it's in an accent that I can't quite make out. All I know is that in this scenario I'm not like him, and he's not like me, and that's more than okay. In fact, it's irrelevant. Had he been just like me, the work wouldn't have gotten done any quicker.

In fact, pretty early on in the day he identifies a way we could work smarter. I've been digging ditches for some time in these parts, and I don't know anyone who does it the way he's suggesting. But it seems a thoughtful approach, so we try it, and it shaves several hours off of the work. So I'm thankful for the fresh eyes he brought to the job.

By day's end we have spanned the whole divide. Without his help it would have taken a full second day of hard labor to get to where we stand today. I express my gratitude, but there is no money in my pockets to pay him for his work, and he maintains that he would have refused it anyway. So I invite him to my home that night for dinner.

It's a humble meal, but everything we have to offer, we gladly share. And it isn't until midway through the meal that he really begins to open up. He shares his story, even the difficult parts, and I'm pleasantly surprised by his vulnerability. His words pour out like they've been bottled up for years, waiting on an invitation to share.

Some of his words are hard to hear. He sees the world differently than I do, and several times I have to bite my tongue to keep from interrupting. But I hear him out, and eventually I manage to see things from his perspective.

We talk until well after midnight. When I walk him out, we shake hands in parting and embrace. Then he's gone.

Had I not invited him to dig the ditch with me—really, had *he* not offered—I never would have known this man, not his name nor his story nor his point of view. And I know I would have been worse off for it.

In the time that it took to dig a ditch, he went from stranger to co-worker to teacher to friend.

It's easy to judge other people's characters and snub or stiff-arm them before even getting to know what makes them tick or where they're coming from. But when you spend hours working hard toward a common goal with someone, your differences and preferences tend to fall by the wayside. Being down in that ditch makes a way for us to gain a new respect for one another. It makes space to really listen.

If I populate my life with people just like me, then my world is going to be mighty small, indeed—maybe one person deep in all directions.

If there are no opposing views, no fresh vantage points, then there is no stretching beyond myself. No growth. No change.

Some people don't want to deal with the inevitable growing pains that accompany change. They will choose comfort over confrontation any day. This kind of thinking actually scares me. Biology (and legendary football coach Lou Holtz) teaches us that we're either growing—that is, changing—or we're dying. And I'm not about to atrophy due to some misguided sense of self-preservation or fear of change.

As Jo and I move through our crazy new life as semi-celebrities, well-meaning people are always telling us, "Please don't change!" And I'm pretty sure what they're saying is that they don't want us to lose our authenticity. I get that for sure. And yet I wince each time someone says it to us.

Guys, listen, we *have* changed. We *are* changing, and we're about to change some more. It is quite literally impossible to build a company or go on national TV or have children and remain the same.

What's never going to change? Our values, our priorities, our commitment to each other and our family. But I hope that literally every other part of our lives changes. I hope that every new season and situation of life changes me.

Some people show enormous resistance to modifying even a fraction of themselves. They're not about to shift the way they think or what they think they know. They simply expect others to get with the program—to adjust their mind-set and fall into their way of thinking. How ignorant for any one of us to assume that we have a monopoly on right perspective and no one else holds even a piece of the puzzle. And how arrogant to just demand that people change for us without ever making the effort to know them as human beings or understand where they're coming from.

I wonder if being angrily shouted at or arrogantly debated with has ever swayed a single person? Are human hearts moved by being ridiculed and mocked? When people fling accusations with the presumption of knowing another person's intentions, what possible outcome could they be hoping for? Who would ever move to their enemy's camp under such treatment?

I really believe that we won't get anywhere, that no healing or breakthrough can occur apart from developing actual relationships with one another. As much as I love Twitter, Twitter feuds aren't going to work. Actually connecting requires true face-to-face time. And that's where the ditch comes in.

I believe with all my heart that it's only after working side by side with another person that you earn the right to speak into that person's life. It's a basis of friendship that can forge a path toward common ground.

The ditch is where trust is built. Then it's at the dining room table, laden with lovingly prepared food, that walls come down. It's around the table that you discover you might, in fact, love this person you were pretty sure you were supposed to hate. It's here that both sides are heard and hearts begin to change. Maybe not wholly. This isn't some manipulative act where the goal is to win someone over to your side. The goal is listening and truly hearing. It's letting your guard down and letting your heart open up. The goal is to leave the table no longer as strangers or enemies, but as fellow travelers on the journey of life. Maybe you even leave as friends who have chosen to agree-to-disagree on some things. This is where hate and fear begin to lose their grip. This is where you begin to have each other's back even when you can't fully embrace each other's cause.

The truth is, we don't have to agree on everything to be friends, but a lot of people—a *lot* of people—seem to think we do. That popular and toxic lie has taken our beautiful planet and turned it into a battleground. The assumption is, *if you don't think like me, not only are you wrong, but you are bad and possibly even evil.*

Judging others' intentions is a nasty business. I'm convinced we do best to steer clear of it entirely. Even just in my own life, I am amazed at the ways that my heart has been misunderstood. It's character assassination, and where I come from a person's most valuable possession is his or her character.

I'm all for disagreeing on the issues. That's the beauty of being unique creatures with differing thoughts, opinions, and perspectives. How boring would it be to all agree on everything? I'm so thankful that there's a whole wide world of individual points of view and we're not some sci-fi tragedy of collective thinking. But when it goes from having opposing viewpoints to actually maligning the other person's character, then there's something wrong. Challenge opinions all day long, but at least save your assessment of who someone is until after you have gotten to know him or her.

It seems to me that we Americans are in an all-out war in this regard. It doesn't feel too terribly far off to think that World War III could break out over just an exchange of words. When contempt has become the norm and misinformation is rampant, it makes way for a kind of rhetoric that may only be silenced by absolutism. Not trying to be an alarmist here, but I am deeply concerned.

Let me lay out my strategy to counter this tendency. Basically, it's a matter of rolling up your sleeves and learning to work with people who don't think the way you do. From there, it's a lot of gathering around dining room tables to eat good food and talk. There's only one rule at these dinners: if you come to share, you also have to come prepared to hear what is being said. Actually, it's not enough to just hear; you must also *listen*.

My hope is that each of these meals would contain long periods of quiet (other than some quiet chewing sounds, some sipping, and strains of the Simon and Garfunkel album playing in the other room) as well as the almost imperceptible sound of hearts being split wide open.

The Bible has quite a bit to say on loving your neighbor, as do nearly all of the sacred texts of the major world religions. But how do we *actually* love our neighbors? I mean, do we even understand who qualifies as our neighbor? Are they the people who live in the homes directly adjacent to us? Are they just the people in our city or maybe the whole country? Or are all the residents of planet Earth considered our neighbors?[1]

I prefer the last answer. I want to live in a world where we are all considered each other's neighbor, where every person's voice matters. I'm convinced that every child on this earth is valuable and worthy of dignity and respect.

There is no chance for any of us to see eye to eye if we are unwilling to even look in each other's direction. Hate masquerading as righteousness can sit in church every Sunday and no one bats an eye. Contempt and judgment clothed in concern says more about "the concerned" than "the concerning," if you catch my drift.

I am thankful to be friends with all types of people—tall, fat, funny, intelligent, not-that-smart, athletic, artistic, and every shade of skin under the sun, plus gay, straight, Muslim, Christian, Buddhist, Jewish, and atheist. Obviously this is not an exhaustive list and it's preposterous for me to suggest that I could be personal friends with every type of person on the planet. But these are some of the common labels that society uses to mark all of us for exclusion. If I had my way, we would all just be considered people.

There are no boxes I'm looking to check by saying that. There's no notch in the belt or pat on the back I'm looking for. I'm simply a better person for knowing lots of different kinds of people. *They* make *me* a better man. If any of these people are ever in a ditch and need a hand, I hope I'm the first person to happen past.

I believe that we are all children of God, the whole lot of us. This means that we are all inherently beautiful, flawed as we are. We all have truth and goodness within us, and our lives were created with intentionality; we were born for a purpose. Every person that you happen upon in your lifetime has a story to tell. Every person on the planet has the ability to teach us, if we'll only be willing to listen.

President Abraham Lincoln famously built a "team of rivals" to advise him—a cabinet filled with people of opposing views and from different political factions.[2] He even included three men in the group who had run directly against him in the election. Where do you think Lincoln's famous "house divided" quote came from? He was living this thing out, and he knew he was better off with people who were willing to challenge his viewpoint. President Lincoln knew that the country would be better served by politicians learning to wrestle beyond the divide than by a homogenous, partisan set of officials always getting their way.

I think we desperately need a "team of rivals," ditch-digging, dinner-table approach to making connections with one another today. I wish it were the norm for Republicans to mostly just tune into CNN and NPR. I wish that Democrats were on a steady diet of Fox News. Mainly, I just wish we would all put ourselves in a position of *listening*. We can yell at the screen, get mad and sad all we want, as long as we engage, hear, and truly try to understand what the other side is fighting for and why. It can only be good for us to stand where they stand, take in the landscape from their perspective for a bit. Rather than ridicule and belittle, we can choose to acknowledge why they are passionate about what they are passionate about.

These battle lines drawn down the center of our country's soul seem to be costing us our humanity. We stereotype and mock entire people groups merely because they think differently or look different than we do. The oversimplified strokes with which we paint perfect strangers isn't just hateful; it's ignorant. If we could get a handle on what this "team of rivals" thing is all about, we just might become formidable in a way that this world has never seen.

Early in 2016 the Elite Café, one of Waco's oldest restaurants, closed down after nearly a hundred years of business. One of its great claims to fame was that it had the honor of feeding Elvis Presley back in the day. When it closed its doors for the last time, I barely hesitated before making an offer on this great piece of real estate. Jo and I have wanted to open up a breakfast joint for a few years now. Hospitality is a big part of what we do at Magnolia, so the restaurant business really seemed to fit.

The Elite Café is a big part of Waco's history, and we wanted to honor that legacy, so we really, really struggled with whether to keep the original name or not. We knew that changing it could be an unpopular decision here in town, and we nearly kept it for that reason alone. But as we considered all that we hoped for this place—what we wanted this new iteration of the old restaurant to be—we quickly realized that the new hope and old name were diametrically opposed.

After much deliberation, we decided to name the café Magnolia Table. We chose this new name because we wanted our restaurant to be a clear representation of a place where *all* are welcome. The former slogan was "Where the elite come to eat." To us the word *elite* speaks of a separation, a divide. Us and them, the haves and the have-nots. We are finding a lot of ways to honor the heritage of the historic café through the renovation, and we are thankful that we get to build upon its legacy with a new rally cry of sorts—one that gives everyone a seat at the table.

I've talked about the dining table as being a place where enemies are lost and friendships are forged, where people really hear each other out. Magnolia Table is our symbolic offering to that cause. We hope it becomes a place where people come to the community table, enjoy great food, and actually talk with the strangers beside them—where instead of worrying about their differences, they find those precious similarities.

Ultimately, we really aren't so different from one another, after all. If we could get back to remembering that, then I think there is some real hope for us yet.

Up until this point in life, I have never given one second of thought to the idea of bridge building. But Joanna and I were pretty dismayed throughout this past election year at how our beloved nation was behaving. It was *bad*. Election years have always been brutal, but this last one was of an entirely different magnitude. The hate and the fear and the overall discord felt tangible.

I remember a night when Jo and I sat up late, talking about what could be done. How do people move beyond party lines, beyond religious affiliation, gender, and race? I remember the conversation coming around to the idea of bridge building.

For as long as we have been together, Jo and I could for sure be accused of being dreamers. We can be idealistic to a fault. And a lot of our late-night ideas and dreams and schemes fall away, even by morning. But this idea of being bridge builders has stuck with us, especially as we turn our thoughts forward to the next chapter of our lives.

This is what we want to do. This is who we want to be.

The idea of bridge building has become something of a mission to us and our team these days. As of late, our midnight planning sessions are spent dreaming up some sort of bridge-building summit, a time and place where people from all kinds of backgrounds and mind-sets come together to help figure out a way forward. It's basically our own version of Abraham Lincoln's cabinet, albeit a lot larger and probably quite a bit rowdier.

A SHORT HISTORY LESSON

WACO SUSPENSION BRIDGE

The fact that I live in a town with a famous bridge of its own is not lost on me. The Waco Suspension Bridge was built back in the late 1800s, when Waco began to rival Dallas in size. Because of the sheer number of people flooding into our city, it became clear that a better means of crossing the Brazos River was necessary. Up until the bridge was built, there was no other way to cross the river for eight hundred miles. So as you can imagine, it attracted people from all over to this one place, simply so they could

---

get to the other side. Such a seemingly simple idea was made possible by this one structure.

The Waco Suspension Bridge was the first of its kind in the whole state, but that didn't make it impossible for the engineer and the men who built it from the ground up. It simply made the work they did that much more important. When it was completed, it was the longest single-span suspension bridge west of the Mississippi! This bridge became a magnet, and even then, it was a symbol of unity. It united both sides of the city, but it also brought all kinds of people together to cross it, even cattle along the Chisholm Trail.

Bridges, when built strong and sure, are powerful to behold—and they change lives.

Building bridges is not a new concept. And although I'm not smart enough to be an engineer even of a figurative bridge like what I am talking about, what I *can* do is put in the hard work to help get it built. I'm happy to do the grunt work. I'm happy to get in the ditch and help build this thing by the sweat of my brow—hopefully side by side with a lot of other ditch diggers. Digging out the foundation for the piers and the beams of a sizable bridge requires a ton of hard work.

I would love to be a part of that. Eventually I want to be able to stand with the engineers and the other ditch diggers and everyone else, point to that beautiful bridge, and say, "I was a part of that."

BRIDGE-BUILDING SUMMIT

Tweet me @chippergaines with any ideas you may have for the bridge-building summit we're working on. We want to hear about the things you feel passionate about and your thoughts on the topic of bridge building in general. Where does the divide affect you personally? When do you feel unheard, unseen, or undervalued? What are you afraid of about the direction we're headed in? What do you think can heal this country, this planet? What messages of hope would you like to share? Also, if you have read a book or watched a film or heard someone speak on a topic that could be valuable to the ongoing effort of building bridges, please send me the name or the link or whatever. We want a fully stocked arsenal of resources as we begin to fight this good fight.

======================================

CHAPTER 15

THE RUNWAY

I've always been taken by the big pecan trees that are on our property. These tall, aged trees are like a welcome committee for us each time we pull up to our farmhouse. I could stand there and marvel at the wonder of them. It's not just their beauty that captivates me—though they are beautiful. I like to think about all that these trees must have seen; the stories they could tell.

Our house was built back in 1885. I like to imagine that the pioneer who built it surveyed the land and intentionally chose this specific spot, nestled between a grove of young pecan trees, to lay the foundation of this home. He recognized their worth. He knew that one day, years from now, they'd grow to provide shade and protection and that eventually they'd produce a bountiful and nutritious harvest. So, he pruned, tended, and watered.

The thing about pecan trees is that they need one to two inches of water a week. So in seasons of drought, he knew these trees wouldn't make it unless he intervened. He had to have known that the harvest would be worth the work. And though their yield would be small during his lifetime, he knew that years down the road those trees would start producing larger quantities of pecans. He knew that the next generation and the generation after that would reap the real harvest.

Now, more than a hundred years later, my family gets to enjoy these massive pecan trees. We get the opportunity to walk down to the pecan grove and picnic under the shade of these magnificent beauties. And every autumn, when the pecans start to fall, the kids run around and gather them up. Jo makes pies, and we all go down to the seed shop to sell the surplus.

That pioneer knew just what he was doing when he chose this spot for our home. He knew the hard work he poured into tending these trees year after year would pay off one day—and it did, even if he wasn't around to see it. He invested in this land even though he knew he would never get the chance to enjoy the full fruits of his labor.

Now that's one heck of a legacy.

As a forty-two-year-old, I find it hard to imagine what my legacy might be or what kind of weight it will hold. I'm too young; I haven't earned it yet. But I do think about it, hoping that someday someone will reap the harvest of what I'm sowing.

None of us is an island. What each of us does today will directly affect somebody else down the road. I'm still reaping the harvest of the folks who have gone before me. I'm still living in the warm light of *their* legacy.

When I'm on my deathbed, I don't want people to only remember me for superficial reasons. I hope that when they think of Chip Carter Gaines, they think of me like a runway—that leveled strip of ground that gives aircraft all the space they need to take off and fly. What drives me these days is the idea of being a launching pad for others, someone who empowers people and believes in them even when they can't quite believe in themselves.

My dream of becoming a runway for folks is not a random notion that just came to me one day. This ideal was modeled for me all of my life. I have seen it lived out, and that has dramatically influenced the kind of person I want to be.

My first "runway" was my granddad, J. B. He exemplified hard work and lived a simple life. Every day he woke up and put on the same boots and the same jeans and drove the same truck. Every day, day in and day out. Even though he wasn't a perfect man, his strengths marked me forever. He instilled in me this unspoken sense of what hard work looks like.

Another inspiration for me is my father-in-law, Jerry. He is a man of few words and abounding grace. He raised Jo with such intentionality. He had everything to do with her becoming the woman of my dreams. He also got behind my dreams of making it as an entrepreneur and gave me the space to try it my own way, even when he knew better.

And the biggest inspiration of all is my father. His character, his integrity, and his faithfulness to our family—these are all parts of the legacy that he has left for me, a legacy that future generations will reap the benefit of.

My dad taught me to be a dad. He's selfless to his core. When I lived at home, he was willing to forgo promotions and advancements at work just to have more time to throw a baseball with me in the evenings. He was teaching me the game, but on another level he was showing me how to be a man and how to be a father. He taught me the importance and value of investing in one's family above anything else.

Dad's belief in me—and the blood, sweat, and tears that he invested in me—was the major runway of my life. It gave me a foundation so firm that when my baseball dream was crushed, I still had a strong foothold. It took me a while to understand this, but what my father gave me was not really about baseball, but about hard work, discipline, and the art of never quitting.

Like my dad did for me, I want to spend my life ensuring that others get to live out their dreams. I want to live my life believing in others in a way that helps them to succeed. I want my everyday actions to have far-reaching effects. It is truly my life's mission to empower people to relentlessly chase after their dreams, no matter the cost. To this I am committed.

I'm actually writing this book in hopes that it can be a runway for you—to make a real impact rather than just filling shelf space or collecting dust. Even if you've never had anyone believe in you—a parent or a coach or a teacher—I hope that in reading these pages you'll recognize that I believe in you, that I am confident you are capable of extraordinary things. I hope you'll be empowered to go do something you never thought you were capable of doing. I hope your story somehow builds on my story and we have a sort of shared legacy.

I've gotten to dream up and start quite a few businesses over the years. I've kept most of these businesses under my wings, but I sold a couple along the way. Take my Wash-n-Fold business, for instance. I started it as a little laundry service for Baylor kids. But the boys who bought it from me took the original idea and made something extraordinary out of it. I never dreamt that it was capable of growing into a big multicampus operation spread over several states. But it did, and they made it happen.

A few years into our marriage, Jo and I had an idea for something that didn't really exist in Waco yet—a collegiate housing development. We bought eleven acres of land to build it on. Then along came a firm who wanted to buy both the land and the concept from us. They took that original idea and implemented it on dozens of campuses across the country.

In regards to both of these particular businesses, the people who bought them from me were able to dream bigger than I ever could have. My part in them wasn't the fancy part, the part that gets or even deserves the recognition. I was the small beginning, and that minor role is still plenty fulfilling to me.

Why try to predict what something is capable of or what it's going to do? Instead, why not just make a runway for ideas to take flight—and then enjoy watching them soar.

As to the business I did keep—Magnolia—I've spent quite a bit of time thinking through what I hope its future will be. Until recently, I just sort of assumed that my biggest goal for Magnolia was for it to continue forward, growing in size and scope. And yes, I do hope for that. I want this company to be sustainable and strong and useful in a way that exceeds people's expectations.

But these days what I want even more is for our employees to know that Jo and I believe in them, that we are championing them. I hope they realize that we want them to dream bigger than they ever have before because that's in *their* best interest. We want them to fulfill their wildest dreams. Magnolia is just the beginning for them, and I want them to know that the sky's the limit.

I am so keenly aware that God has entrusted us with Magnolia for a reason. This little company has always meant more to us than any amount of notoriety or recognition ever could. Magnolia will undoubtedly be an enduring part of what we leave behind. We pray that it will far outlast us. We dream that our children's children will get to see what we've built and that it would be a monument symbolizing the value of finding joy in hard work.

Joanna and I also strive every day for the work that we do to create lasting, meaningful, and positive change in our people and our community. We want our employees to rise up as leaders in their own right. We want them to follow their dreams, whatever they may be—go back to school and get that degree, become world-renowned in their fields, or stay home with their children, if that's what they feel they're called to do.

Even if the company loses our valued employees to these dreams of theirs, that's okay. It was our honor to be the runway for them, the launching pad that they needed to go for it. From there we're anticipating a chain reaction of sorts with exponential impact. We believe our employees will go on to change the world in ways that Jo and I could never attain by ourselves. Our legacy is their legacy and vice versa.

I am a father and husband and I always will be, no two ways about it. At the end of the day, I want my four kiddos to know that they are free to do whatever is in their hearts and that they are capable of accomplishing anything they could ever imagine. There's no cap to the amount of time or resources I would give to my kids if I knew it could help them fulfill their destiny. I want to instill in them that they are competent to go do anything in the whole wide world if they are willing to do the work and set their minds to it. And I am confident they'll blow any of my biggest dreams out of the water.

Jo and I have no artificial expectations for our kids—no desire to force them into any particular occupation. In fact, one of the great joys of parenting for us has been to watch our little ones start to come into their own as individuals. It's fun to watch their personalities begin to come into focus along with their own unique talents and preferences.

All Jo and I hope to be as parents are careful stewards of our children. We want to observe them and then slowly and carefully help them identify their God-given gifts. We want to get behind their dreams, and if those change over time, we want to keep evolving right along with them. Whatever they choose to do—large or small, in the foreground or hidden—we will help them navigate that journey.

As parents, we have the unique opportunity to champion our children's dreams in a way that no one else can. We can instill in them the truth that no matter what they choose to do in life, they can change the world. And as long as they know, without a shadow of a doubt, that I gave them a long runway for takeoff, then I'll be satisfied.

CHAPTER 16

GO GET 'EM

For as long as I can remember, I thought I was going to die young—younger than I am now. Maybe that's why I've worked so hard, so fast, and so diligently. And maybe that's why I started working at such a young age. I was racing some invisible clock.

I found this death calculator online (I know, morbid). Based on my height, weight, and body mass index (BMI), along with the fact that I'm pretty active and a nonsmoker, I am estimated to leave this earth on June 16, 2056. I will be eighty-one years old.

Once you see it in black and white like that, life takes on a bit of a different hue. You start to think about how your obituary would read. (I really encourage you to do this—it's fascinating, or intriguing, or eerie, to say the least. And it really brings things into focus.)

Here's one possibility I came up with:

Waco—Chip Carter Gaines, 81, died Friday, June 16, 2056, at 8:36 p.m., alone in his hospital bed. He leaves behind his former wife,

Joanna Stevens, and their four children: Drake Stevens, Ella Rose, Duke Camden, and Emmie Kay Carter.

Chip's marriage ended in a bitter divorce after an unfortunate run as an ongoing celebrity player in the World Series of Poker. Unbeknownst to his wife, he gambled away the entirety of his estate, causing the collapse of his beloved company, Magnolia Inc. The financial infidelity proved more than she could bear. Overcome with shame, he distanced himself from his children, convinced they were better off without him because of his tainted legacy.

Chip grew up as a golden child and lived a charmed life early on. He was a baseball standout in high school, graduated from Baylor University's Hankamer School of Business, and enjoyed a successful career before his downward spiral began. His short-lived foray into D-list television culminated in a brief appearance on *Celebrity Apprentice*, from which he was eliminated before the first week for insubordination and public urination. Penniless, Chip faded away to live out his life in complete obscurity.

Or instead, it could read something like this:

Waco—Chip Carter Gaines, 81, died Friday, June 16, 2056, at 8:36 p.m. at his family's estate, surrounded by loved ones, who were there to usher him into eternity. He leaves behind his beloved wife of fifty-three years, Joanna, and his four children, whom he adored: Drake Stevens, real-estate tycoon and president of Magnolia, Inc.; Ella Rose, world-renowned interior decorator and style maven; Duke Camden, international luxury real-estate architect and developer; and Emmie Kay Carter, acting CEO of Magnolia Omnimedia; as well as their supportive spouses, his sixteen grandchildren, and countless dear friends.

Born in Albuquerque, New Mexico, the son of Robert Kenneth and Beverly Gayle Gaines, he made his home in Waco, Texas, while attending Baylor University and remained there as a lifelong resident and ardent advocate for the city he so loved.

In his early years, Chip excelled in athletics, playing both base-ball and football until he graduated from Grapevine High. He was the team captain for both sports his senior year. He attended Baylor's Hankamer School of Business (later named Gaines International School of Business in his honor), and graduated in 1998 with a busi-ness degree with an emphasis on marketing. He and Joanna Lea Stevens were married at Waco's historic Earle Harrison house in 2003. Later that same year, they opened a small home-decor store called Magnolia, which grew in size and scope over the next few decades, culminating in a cultural phenomenon in the second half of the cen-tury. For four of those years they were featured on a popular television reality show called *Fixer Upper*.

In 2017, Chip and Joanna started the Magnolia Foundation, a nonprofit focused on providing orphan care, youth development, family housing, and community restoration. Over the course of the last thirty-nine years, the funds raised by the foundation have made massive strides in helping to solve child homelessness and provid-ing world-class entrepreneurial training for at-risk youth. Chip also devoted many hours campaigning and working to lower the poverty rate of his beloved city, and by the time of his death, it had been suc-cessfully lowered to 6 percent.

In 2040, Chip's bride, Joanna, won a surprise victory in the pres-idential general election as the first female half Korean to take the oval office. She went on to win a second term. Chip was her running mate and two-term vice president. Though he never acknowledged it, Chip was largely credited with the successful campaign strategies of criminalizing fear-based living and creating a comprehensive strategy for bridge building.

In addition to his political contributions, Chip was a lifelong lover of animals, babies, and world peace. He also loved to run, and from age forty-two to eighty-one, he completed sixteen marathons and par-ticipated in four IronMan triathlons. An avid humanitarian, he toured the globe as an agent of reconciliation and an ambassador of hope.

After his second attempt at retirement, Chip spent the last decade of his life teaching Spanish-as-a-second-language (SSL) in Playa del Carmen to aspiring entrepreneurs.

His ashes are being scattered at the Gaines estate outside of Waco, in the southernmost pasture. In lieu of flowers, please make a donation to the Magnolia Foundation in his memory.

SPOILER ALERT: WE ALL DIE

I don't care what your death calculator says, whether you're estimated to live nine years or ninety-nine. From heaven's perspective, it all happens in the blink of an eye. And death happens to every one of us.

I'm not afraid to die. But I'm also not afraid to live. I'm not sure which of these two possibilities scares folks more, but I'm guessing it's the *really living* one. Death is just an instant in time. But life is one million choices, one million chances to go all-in, up the ante, double down, or cash out. To keep choosing to go all-in, day after day, can sound exhausting and scary. But stick with me here.

The world is full of people who choose the safe and predictable path. They save for their 401(k)s and work their fingers to the bone, focused on climbing the corporate ladder all the way to the tippy top. These people spend a considerable amount of time checking off all these invisible boxes. They live in fear that if they don't do this, that, and the other to ensure their security, something bad will happen to them. It's the monster lurking in the closet, the thing that goes bump in the night. They can't quite put their finger on it, but that doesn't mean it's not out there.

It's been said that most adults make around thirty-five thousand conscious choices every single day—a staggering number.[1] And each one of those decisions has the ability to direct our paths one way or another. So many things can affect them too. Hunger, fatigue, mood, our spouse's mood, the weather—any of it can play a part. And I'd bet that a good percentage of many people's decisions are made simply because they provide the path of least resistance.

Boo.

Unfortunately, I think most of us have become subconsciously obsessed with safety and comfort and make our choices accordingly. The problem with that is that nothing worthwhile comes easy. So behind almost every one of those decisions we make is an even bigger decision, the compass that determines the direction of our lives:

- Do I want a safe, comfortable, and easy life?
- Or do I want my days to matter?

I'm guessing that at the end of most people's lives, they're not wishing they'd passed on more promotions or that they'd spent less time with their families. More likely, they're grappling with whether or not they made a true impact on the world.

I know I'll be asking the same question of myself: How many people's lives were actually better off because theirs intersected with my own?

So I'm urging you (and myself as well) to find something worthwhile in this one invaluable life of yours. Find something to fight for. Something to *live* for.

You may already know the thing that you were created for, and you may already be getting after it. If that's your story, I salute you for making things happen. I get excited thinking about a world where everyone is living out their dreams for the greater good. But it terrifies me to think that we might very well live in a world with more armchair critics than torchbearers.*

I value both logic and passion. To me they are both essential.

Logic serves in many critical ways, helping keep us organized and make sensible decisions. But there is one job that it is utterly ineffective

---

* An armchair critic is someone who sits on their comfy couch (or armchair) and criticizes people who are creating and moving rather than creating or moving themselves. But a torchbearer is someone who is on the move, leading or inspiring others in working toward a valued goal.

at. It cannot provide powerful motivation. That's what passion is for. Even if your passion is to be an accountant—arguably the most logical career you can choose—logic isn't what stirs you as you create spread-sheets and analyze numbers. Passion is.

A logical approach makes a strong case for a safe major at a respected university. It paves the way for a high-paying job due to your sought-after skill set. Logic alone is not enough to convince you to be an artist, but a passion for art may well motivate you to go that direction. Any well-intentioned dad will tell you that seeking a career in art is impractical, but it sure wasn't for Picasso.

Yes, it may be hard to find a job after graduation. The word most commonly associated with *artist* is *starving*, after all. So why on earth would you consider it as a career?

Because of passion. Because that little voice, the one not swayed by fear, is encouraging you to get after it.

Passion is the thing that reminds you that no matter how seemingly unlikely, your art could impart something important to our planet. That using your God-given talent can't *not* improve the plight of mankind. That's why talents are called gifts—because they're meant to be shared.

When you combine this kind of bold bravery with a calling you're passionate about, you become a force to be reckoned with.

Finding your passion may not be as easy as it sounds. A lot of people simply have no clue to what they want to give their precious life—or at the very least, their time. If that's true, let me see if I can help out a little.

Take a look at some of the different facets of society:

- government
- science
- technology
- education
- family
- economy
- military

- faith/religion
- media
- business
- sports
- arts and entertainment

It doesn't take a genius to recognize that each of these categories—each and every aspect of our world—has some real room for improvement.

Read through that list again, more slowly this time. Do any of these resonate with you? Maybe you feel angry about the current state of affairs in one (or more) of these categories. Or maybe when you were a kid you dreamed of working in one of these specific fields.

Any emotion that is stirred in you by this exercise is not random. These feelings are smoke signals, and where there's smoke, there's fire.

People tend to associate fire with something negative, but fire is the palpable ingredient of passion. Fire is cleansing energy, a channel for a fresh start. For change.

When you think of a forest fire rolling through miles and miles of overgrown trees and brush, think of it like this. After an event like that, the nutrients in trees and plants are burned into ash and then are returned to the soil to support new growth. Brush and weeds are cleared to make way for smaller trees to thrive without competition. Harmful insects and diseases are wiped out. Sunlight is able to reach the forest floor, which means wildflowers will begin popping through in places that haven't seen new life in years. I'm getting at the fact that a fire sometimes burns away the unnecessary to make room for the beautiful.

If there's something stirring in you now, and you know what it is, do *that*. There's no need to overthink it. A mistake here and there isn't going to kill you, so don't waste time worrying about that. It's infinitely better to fail with courage than to sit idle with fear, because only one of these gives you the slightest chance to live abundantly. And if you do fail, then the worst-case scenario is that you'll learn something from it. You're for sure not going to learn jack squat from sitting still and playing it safe.

There's actual, real work to do, and now's the time to do it. Not one of us is getting any younger, and waiting for your "perfect moment" or for the "most convenient time" could very well turn into a missed opportunity. You've been given everything you need to call the shots and to make things happen. You were built for this, so get to work.

If you are working in a cubicle at some company, shuffling from meeting to meeting, and you feel invisible, then go find something that inspires you, something you can give yourself to after you punch out for the day. The quality of the work that you do from eight to five will reflect that decision.

You may be in your sixties, feeling that you've missed your shot. If your death calculator is anything like mine, you still have a good couple of decades to spare. It's not too late. Until the buzzer rings, it ain't over. No one is disqualified.

I believe each one of you still has important things to do, or you wouldn't still be here on this earth. Hear me now: if you are able to read this book, you are able to change the world. It might be through small, everyday choices, but those initial sparks can set the whole world on fire.

As for me, all I've ever wanted, when you get right down to it, is to change the world. I don't literally mean the whole wide world. That would be nice, I guess, but what I really care about is changing the world around me. This means pouring into the lives of my wife and my kids, my employees, my friends, and my acquaintances. That's the ripple effect I've always hoped to put into motion.

Rather than taking the easy way out, I learned to trust myself.

That voice we hear when we're thinking about going out on a limb— tune into it.

There's one thing I want to leave with you: trusting your gut is the first step. Although that first step won't be enough to get you across the finish line, it's definitely the hardest—and the most important—of every single one that follows. Plus, once you've started, you won't want to stop. Momentum, remember?

Complacency is the enemy, and getting started is as triumphant as crossing the finish line. Your goal is too far off to have a straight line of sight to it, but I'm going to need you to keep it firmly fixed in your mind's eye. The only way this is going to work, the only way that you're gonna get there, is one foot in front of the other. You have to keep moving forward. And when you think you are about to die—trust me, it's just a tiny bit further.

All of your life has been prepping you for this moment in time. I get that you may not know what your next chapter holds. I don't know what mine holds either. For Jo and me, the future is nothing but blank pages before us. But we have already started writing on them.

Thanks for taking the time to read my story. And if you will, make me one commitment. Live a life worthy of being written down, so that at the next go-round, I'm reading *your* story.

I can't wait to hear it!

what are you waiting for?
Go get 'em!

What do workers gain from their toil? I have seen the burden God has laid on the human race. He has made everything beautiful in its time. He has also set eternity in the human heart; yet no one can fathom what God has done from beginning to end. I know that there is nothing better for people than to be happy and to do good while they live. That each of them may eat and drink, and find satisfaction in all their toil—this is the gift of God.

ECCLESIASTES 3:9–13

WRITE IT DOWN HERE RIGHT NOW

Okay, now you've finished the book. Here's what I want you to do next.

Find one thing, one word, or one phrase in this book that speaks to you. Circle it and reflect on it. Why did that stand out to you? What is that voice inside of you trying to say?

Don't let fear bury it. If you let it sit still for too long, the fire is going to get stomped out by what-ifs.

Now write down what you're passionate about or what inspires you. Write it here. Right now. How are you going to get there? What practical steps are you going to take? Write those down too. Even if you can only think of one, write it down.

Next time we cross paths, I expect to see progress. What're you waiting for? Get writing!

_____

_____

_____

_____

_____

NOTES

NOTES

FROM THE DESK OF CHIP GAINES

I've had a handful of personal assistants over the years, and each of them, for various reasons, has changed my life for the better. Funny, because when word got out that I was writing this book, they each insisted that I let them speak their mind. I have no idea what they could be so desperate to tell the world, and I'm still not convinced that these things warrant space in this book, but alas, a promise is a promise.

Behold, here are some of their accounts.

ELIZABETH

When I went in for my interview, all I really wanted was a quaint part-time job at this new trendy store in town. I remember Jo talking about what Chip needed: "He likes good communication," she said. "Always reply to every single text message with at least an 'okay' or a 'got it.' He needs you to show initiative, drive, and a can-do attitude."

I went back to meet with Chip at two in the afternoon, and our interview didn't end until around five, when everyone was leaving the office for the day. I barely spoke during the entire interview. (Chip remembers me as shy and mute.) I remember Chip using lawyers and football coaches as metaphors for most of the points he made. I'm not sure if he even asked me any questions. I think he just talked to me the whole time like a coach: "Hey, kiddo, here's what it's like here. Here's what you need to do this job well."

I remember Chip would come in during filming breaks and give office-wide pep talks. Usually, his first stop was the design girls, and then he'd come sit in my office, take off his insanely stinky ten-year-old boots, throw them into the hallway, and put his feet up on my desk. He'd literally heckle me, listening to me answer the phone and even sometimes taking some calls himself. He'd ask about the e-mails I was getting, wave to people in the shop windows, and get up to take photos with them. Oh, and of course he'd tweet nonstop.

He quickly proved his integrity and his love for people. He took every opportunity to be kind and generous, to encourage his family, and to invest in those around him. He is a true discipler. He doesn't take the quick road. He gets into the mud with people and helps them grow. He wants to see people succeed. He celebrates people when they surpass their own expectations. And those are just a few of the really special things about Chip.

Once Chip was out of town for the weekend, and he left me with a few "simple" tasks. He wanted me to get him a loan, buy a houseboat and preferably a couple of Jet Skis, too, and get the boat docked in Lake Waco in a slip on the end of the dock.

Spending someone else's money on big, important things like that is scary. The bank was giving me a hard time with the loan, but I knew Chip wouldn't take no for an answer. I was literally one stressful phone call away from taking the money out of my personal savings account. I was still so new and wasn't in a position to mess this up. I remember running all around Lake Waco begging people for the boat slip. Actually getting the boat to the marina was a whole other ordeal. But somehow or other it all ended up working out, and I didn't get myself fired on that one.

While on a trip to New York, Chip and Jo had seen some crazy nice apartment for sale. He called me and said, "Okay, Elizabeth, I need you to take this very seriously. Call these guys and find out how much this apartment is listed for. If you sound like you don't know what you're talking about, they won't talk to you. If you don't sound like an adult, they will hang up on you. You have to sound like a grown-up real-estate professional."

Oh, crap. I have the voice of a thirteen-year-old, and I don't know what I'm talking about. But no way was I going to fail this challenge. I called my dad and had him tell me exactly what I should say to make these guys take me seriously. So full of nerves, and wanting to get this right, I called the listing agent. We talked, and he gave me the price, which was something like forty million dollars. So I texted Chip and gave him that message. His response? "Well, shoot. I owe Jo five bucks." Really? I'd been stressing over this big assignment, and it was all over a bet with Jo?

One day Chip was in the office and heard the music duo Johnnyswim's song "Home" playing in the store. As far as I know, this was the first time he had heard the song, and he thought it would be perfect for the opening of the show. He told me, "Get that song as our theme song."

I e-mailed Sony and got a reply! I ended up on the phone with a Sony rep, then with Johnnyswim's agent, and then with Abner and Amanda (the members of Johnnyswim) themselves. Abner's family were fans of the show, and they thought it would be so fun to have their song as the theme song.

I called Chip and told him the good news. He asked me how much it was going to cost, and I thought, *Oh, I didn't even ask them about a price, but they are fans, and they want to be on the show.* So I told Chip it was going to be free.

He said, "No way."

"Yeah," I told him, "for sure it's free."

He said, "Elizabeth, Sony is not going to give us a song for free. Call them back and ask the price." I was embarrassed to ask, but I did it.

Turns out it was *not* free. It was *really* not free. I hated to call Chip back and tell him I was wrong and admit how naive I was, but thankfully he just chalked it up to a learning experience.

"Get Dolly pregnant" was on my to-do list for *months*. Chip had a horse that he wanted to have bred, and this became my personal responsibility. With the help of a breeder, a stud, and months of horse matchmaking, she finally got pregnant! I'm not going to lie to you, but the length of detail that the vet went into when he explained things had me blushing for weeks.

Chip is a saint. I literally didn't know anything about anything when I was hired, and he was the most gracious person during my time at Magnolia. He taught me *so* much. I truly credit him for helping me grow up, and he literally made me feel like I could do anything.

RICHARD

Once, Chip had me go buy a pig for him. When I got back to the farm, I let the pig out in the pasture with the other animals, and he immediately ran away. I spent half the night trying to find this animal and was sure he had been eaten by coyotes. Probably not my best first impression as Chip's assistant.

Probably the most stomach-dropping moment was the time I accidentally sent a direct message to Steve Forbes from Chip's Twitter account. Maybe it wasn't *that* big of a deal, but Chip's Twitter is like a woman's purse. You don't mess with it.

Speaking of Twitter, once Chip tweeted out that I was single and that everyone should follow me. Embarrassing. I had multiple grandmothers send me pictures of their granddaughters.

Oh, and more animal purchases. He had me buy goats. And then more goats. Then he asked me to breed the goats. This was a *big* learning experience for me.

BETH

I get asked the question all the time, "What's it like working for Chip? Is he as funny in real life as he is on TV?" The answer to that question is a resounding yes!

I remember my first day of work. Joanna was out of the office working on the finishing touches for a *Fixer Upper* house. Chip welcomed me to Magnolia, and we chatted in the office for a while. He told me to take it easy for the first six months or so of employment so that I could learn my way around and get acquainted with people. After that we would really get to work. I was thinking to myself, *Noooooo! Six months with nothing to do? I will die of boredom if they don't give me any work!*

I need not have worried. Less than twenty minutes later he bounded out of the office and gave me my first assignment. "Never mind on the six-month wait," he said. "I need you to register our chickens with the Texas Department of Poultry so my girls can sell baby chicks."

Did I hear him right? Chickens? Yep, that's right. Before I knew it, I had made arrangements to meet with the poultry inspector at the farm so that the chicks could be approved for sale. And that's how the wild adventure of working for Chip began.

I never know what I'll be doing for Chip from day to day. One day he came flying through the office door, running late for a meeting. He called to me and said, "Beth, it's kind of a long story, but I picked up a homeless guy, and he's sitting outside in the parking lot. Can you go out there, talk to him, and find him a job?" And off he went into his meeting.

With a little trepidation, I walked outside and met "Mike" (not his real name). He told me his story, and I asked him what kind of work experience he had. He was down on his luck, but I really believed there was hope for this guy. I called the warehouse manager, and we set up a plan to find him a job. We even scheduled an interview.

Unfortunately, Mike's story did not end well. Despite our making every effort and giving him several chances, he never showed up for an interview, and we lost touch with him. But even though this endeavor did not turn out like we hoped, it was worth the effort. You never know; Chip might have been the only person to ever believe in him. Someday Mike might be ready to make a change and remember that someone gave him a chance.

Within my first week of work, Chip asked me if I had a Twitter account. I had never really used Twitter and didn't know much about it. Chip told me I better get set up and quickly because he loves to use Twitter to connect with people. With a little help from our social media director, my account was set up, and that's when I became @assistingchip.

Chip's Twitter giveaways quickly became one of my favorite things about working for him. He has given away everything from all-expenses paid trips to Waco to a Jimmy Don (Holmes) sign that someone saw on the show and loved. T-shirts, hats, Demo Day hammers, concert tickets, Broadway tickets in New York City, school tuition—whatever captures his attention is fair game for a giveaway. I love to make these things happen, and the joy that they bring to people makes me so happy. It feels like Christmas all year round!

Working for both Chip and Joanna is a real juggling act. As their executive assistant I manage many aspects of their business and personal lives, from working with producers on the filming schedule to meeting with executives, making last-minute travel plans, and taking care of their vehicles and home projects. Every day is different, and there is never a dull moment!

One time Joanna was getting ready to go out of town for a meeting, and she asked me to have some work done on her car to get it ready to sell while she was gone. I scheduled the appointment and dropped off the car to have it repaired. Later that day Chip called and asked me what was happening with her vehicle. I relayed Joanna's instructions to take it to the shop, and Chip told me to hold off on that repair for the time being. When I explained that Joanna wanted this done, he gave an interesting answer that made me laugh. As only Chip could do, he exclaimed, "Welcome to our world! People are always asking us who's in charge, and the answer is, when Jo is gone, I'm the boss."

NOTES

CHAPTER 3: LOST IN TRANSLATION

1. Oxford Living Dictionaries: English, s.v. "delusional," accessed July 23, 2017, https://en.oxforddictionaries.com/definition/delusional.

2. You can find it in Luke 15:11–32 in the New Testament. If you don't have a Bible, BibleGateway.com is an excellent resource. You can find one version of this story at https://www.biblegateway.com/passage/?search=Luke+15%3A11–32&version=NIV.

CHAPTER 6: FEAR-LESS

1. "North Korea's Nuclear Weapons: Here Is All We Know," *Al Jazeera*, May 30, 2017, http://www.aljazeera.com/news/2017/05/north-korea-testing-nuclear-weapons-17-5-4-82226461.html.

2. Martin Chulov, "Sarin Used in April Syria Attack, Chemical Weapons Watchdog Confirms," *The Guardian*, June 30, 2017, https://www.theguardian.com/world/2017/jun/30/sarin-was-used-in-syria-khan-sheikhun-attack-says-chemical-weapons-watchdog.

3. Nathanial Gronewold, "One Quarter of World's Population Lacks Electricity," *Scientific American*, November 24, 2009, https://www.scientificamerican.com/article/electricity-gap-developing-countries-energy-wood-charcoal/.

4. Amanda Chan, "The 10 Deadliest Cancers and Why There's No Cure," Live Science, September 10, 2010, https://www.livescience.com/11041-10-deadliest-cancers-cure.html.

5. Christopher Maloney, answer posted to the question "How Many Different Diseases Are Known to Exist That Affect at Least 1% of the People in the U.S. at Some Point in Their Lives?" Quora, April 7, 2015, https://www.quora.com/How-many-different-diseases-are-known-to-exist-that-affect-at-least-1-of-the-people-in-the-U-S-at-some-point-in-their-lives. For more information, see National Center for Health Statistics, "International Classification of Diseases, (ICD-10-CM/PCS) Transition—Background," Centers for Disease Control and Prevention, page updated October 1, 2015, https://www.cdc.gov/nchs/icd/icd10cm_pcs_background.htm.

6. Christian Alliance for Orphans, "On Understanding Orphan Statistics," Christian Alliance for Orphans' White Paper, October 20, 2015, 3, https://cafo.org/wp-content/uploads/2015/10/Orphan-Statistics-Web-9-2015.pdf. These numbers were derived from information published by UNICEF, UNAIDS, and WHO in 2010.

7. United Nations International Children's Emergency Fund, "Goal: Reduce Child Mortality," UNICEF Millennium Development Goals, accessed July 20, 2017, https://www.unicef.org/mdg/childmortality.html.

8. Ibid.

9. Michael Graham Richard, "87% of Earth's Population Lives Where the Air Is Toxic," Treehugger.com, December 9, 2015, https://www.treehugger.com/natural-sciences/87-earths-population-lives-areas-where-air-toxic.html.

10. Laura Ungar and Mark Nichols, "4 Million Americans Could Be Drinking Toxic Water and Would Never Know: A USA Today Network Investigation," *USA Today*, December 13, 2016, https://www.usatoday.com/story/news/2016/12/13/broken-system-means-millions-of-rural-americans-exposed-to-poisoned-or-untested-water/94071732/.

11. Aline Brosh McKenna and Cameron Crowe (screenplay) and Benjamin Mee (book), *We Bought a Zoo*, dir. Cameron Crowe (20th Century Fox, 2011). Quotation found at *"We Bought a Zoo* Quotes," IMDb.com, http://www.imdb.com/title/tt1389137/trivia?tab=qt&ref_=tt_trv_qu.

CHAPTER 10: WACKO, TEXAS

1. Elizabeth Abrahamsen, "Why Waco Is Becoming One of Texas's Hottest Cities," Wide Open Country, accessed July 20, 2017, http://www.wideopencountry.com/how-did-waco-become-one-of-texas-hottest-cities/.

CHAPTER 11: SCRAPPY IS AS SCRAPPY DOES

1. *Urban Dictionary*, s.v. "scrappy," by preshere, June 19, 2008, http://www. urbandictionary.com/define.php?term=scrappy.

2. Sean Kim, "How to Remember 90% of Everything You Learn," Lifehack, May 12, 2016, http://www.lifehack.org/399140/how-to-remember-90-of-everything-you-learn. This information is reportedly based on the Learning Pyramid, published by the NTL Institute of Bethel, Maine, in the early 1960s. For more information, see Wilda V. Heard, "What Is the Learning Pyramid," *DrWilda* (blog), March 6, 2013, https://drwilda. com/2013/03/06/what-is-the-learning-pyramid/.

CHAPTER 12: NEVER QUIT YOUR DAY DREAM

1. David K. William, "Science Proves Funny People Are More Intelligent," Lifehack, accessed July 20, 2017, http://www.lifehack.org/344730/science-proves-funny-people-are-more-intelligent.

CHAPTER 13: SEASON FINALE

1. Actually, Newton's cradle demonstrates *three* fundamental principles of physics—conservation of energy, conservation of momentum, and friction. For an easy-to-understand explanation of how it all works, see Chris Schulz, "How Newton's Cradles Work," HowStuffWorks. com, January 17, 2012, http://science.howstuffworks.com/innovation/inventions/newtons-cradle.htm.

2. This story can be found in Genesis 22:1–19 in the Old Testament. One version can be found online at https://www.biblegateway.com/passage/?search=Genesis+22%3A1–19&version=NIV.

3. This is taken from Job 1:21 in the Bible. One version can be found at https://www.biblegateway.com/passage/?search=Job+1%3A21&version=NIV.

4. Look for this story in chapter 16 of the book of Exodus in the Bible, https://www.biblegateway.com/passage/?search=Exodus+16&version=NIV.

CHAPTER 14: TEAM OF RIVALS

1. Jesus actually answered this question directly by telling a story. If you are curious, you can find it in the Bible—Luke 10:25–37, or https://www. biblegateway.com/passage/?search=luke+10%3A25–37&version=NIV.

2. The term "team of rivals" is taken from the title of a book by Pulitzer Prize–winning historian Doris Kearn Goodwin, who profiled the relationship between Lincoln and his very disparate group of advisors. See Doris Kearn Goodwin, *Team of Rivals: The Political Genius of Abraham Lincoln* (New York: Simon & Schuster, 2005).

CHAPTER 16: GO GET 'EM

1. Jim Sollisch, "The Cure for Decision Fatigue," *Wall Street Journal*, June 10, 2016, https://www.wsj.com/articles/the-cure-for-decision-fatigue-1465596928.

ABOUT THE AUTHOR

Chip Gaines and his wife, Joanna Gaines, are co-founders and co-owners of Magnolia Homes, Magnolia Market, and Magnolia Realty in Waco, Texas. Together, they also host HGTV's *Fixer Upper*, where Chip handles construction and Joanna serves as the lead designer.

Chip was born in Albuquerque, New Mexico, and was raised in Dallas, Texas. He graduated from Baylor University's Hankamer School of Business with a degree in marketing. Chip is an entrepreneur by nature, and started and sold many small businesses before Magnolia. Having grown up spending time on his granddad's ranch in North Texas, Chip became a true cowboy at heart. He says he was made for hard labor and always preferred digging ditches to academic pursuits.

Chip specializes in making the impossible possible for Joanna's designs, and his design preference is "whatever Joanna likes." To say he adds comic relief to their construction team would be an understatement.

Chip loves life with his four kiddos and is head over heels for Joanna. Hand in hand is exactly how Chip prefers to work, and he enjoys seeing his and Joanna's passions merge to complement and serve one another.